D0200021

SENTINEL

A SIMPLE CHRISTMAS

Mike Huckabee hosts the popular talk shows *Huckabee* on Fox News Channel and *The Mike Huckabee Show* each weekday on Cumulus Radio, and presents "The Huckabee Report" commentary three times daily on 600 radio stations. He served as lieutenant governor of Arkansas from 1993 to 1996 and as governor from 1996 to 2007. During the 2008 presidential race he came in second place for the Republican nomination. Mike Huckabee's previous books include *The New York Times* best-sellers *Do the Right Thing, A Simple Christmas*, and *A Simple Government*. His latest book, *Dear Chandler, Dear Scarlett*, is a collection of heart-warming letters to his grandchildren on faith, family, and the things that matter most.

A Simple Christmas

Twelve Stories
That Celebrate the
True Holiday Spirit

Mike Huckabee

SENTINEL

SENTINEL
Published by the Penguin Group
Penguin Group (USA) Inc., 375 Hudson Street, New York, New York 10014, U.S.A.
Penguin Group (Canada), 90 Eglinton Avenue East, Suite 700, Toronto, Ontario,
Canada M4P 2Y3 (a division of Pearson Penguin Canada Inc.)
Penguin Books Ltd, 80 Strand, London WC2R 0RL, England
Penguin Ireland, 25 St. Stephen's Green, Dublin 2, Ireland (a division of Penguin Books Ltd)
Penguin Group (Australia), 707 Collins Street, Melbourne, Victoria 3008, Australia
(a division of Pearson Australia Group Pty Ltd)
Penguin Books India Pvt Ltd, 11 Community Centre, Panchsheel Park, New Delhi – 110 017, India
Penguin Group (NZ), 67 Apollo Drive, Rosedale, Auckland 0632,
New Zealand (a division of Pearson New Zealand Ltd)
Penguin Books, Rosebank Office Park, 181 Jan Smuts Avenue, Parktown North 2193, South Africa
Penguin China, B7 Jiaming Center, 27 East Third Ring Road North,
Chaoyang District, Beijing 100020, China

Penguin Books Ltd, Registered Offices:
80 Strand, London WC2R 0RL, England

First published in the United States of America by Sentinel,
a member of Penguin Group (USA) Inc. 2009
This paperback edition published 2012

1   3   5   7   9   10   8   6   4   2

Illustrations by Charles Waller

ISBN 978-1-59523-062-1 (hc.)
ISBN 978-1-59523-098-0 (pbk.)

Printed in the United States of America
Set in Warnock Pro
Designed by Amy Hill

Once you read this book, you'll understand why I have to dedicate it to members of my family. I do hope they will all still speak to me and invite me to future family gatherings even though they might fear ending up in a future book or even the movie version of this one, which I'm certain Hollywood will want to make.

So to all my family—wife, kids, sister, cousins, aunts and uncles, in-laws, outlaws, and dogs—my thanks for giving me volumes of material to use for this Christmas memoir.

Most of all, thanks to God, who gave us the best Christmas of all when he delivered His love for us in person in the form of the baby in Bethlehem, Jesus.

Contents

Preface

"I'll be home for Christmas" is more than a classic Bing Crosby song—it's the sentiment most of us have as December 25 approaches each year. No matter what we do or where we are, there is something inside us that says that we need to be home for Christmas.

There's something about being home with family and friends that gives us grounding, a sense of place and perspective that provides stability in what might otherwise be a chaotic and turbulent world. This is especially true at Christmas, which is the one time of year when we confront who we are—I mean who we *really* are. By observing the traditions of the season, we are able to look back at where we came from and realize just how far we've come. We spend time with our family and remember that they are people connected to us not just through our DNA but also by memories and experiences that shaped our lives from their earliest moments. Even though the annual trek home is more painful than pleasant for some people, there is still some magnetic force that compels us to fight crowds, traffic, delays, and inconveniences just to make it home for Christmas.

For me this pull was never as strong as it was during the Christmas of 2008. It was a few days before Christmas, and I was in New York, having just finished working on that week's production schedule for my new television show on the Fox News Channel. I was eager to get home for Christmas and had determined that, like a postal worker, neither hail, nor sleet, nor snow was going to keep me from being delivered to my doorstep in North Little Rock, Arkansas.

Don't get me wrong—New York City is a truly magical place, especially at Christmas, when some of the world's most beautiful holiday displays are set up all around Times Square, at Rockefeller Center, and throughout the city. I suppose if a person had to be stuck somewhere for Christmas, New York would be about as decent a place as any, but I didn't want to be stuck anywhere—not even in New York. I had a simple quest—I wanted to get *home*. I wasn't looking for a star-studded, glitzy New York Christmas. I wanted a *simple* Christmas at home with my family. I didn't think this was too much to ask, and God help those who stood in my way!

New York City was a complete mess. Snow and ice had traffic snarled, and flights were being canceled out of all of the airports serving the city. It was the weekend before Christmas, and I had flown into the city on Friday, December 21, after a week in the Bahamas, where my family and I had gone to spend a few days of rest. I needed those few days! It had been a whirlwind year. I won the Iowa caucuses in my bid to become president and came in second while trying to win the GOP nomination. In March John McCain secured the nomination, and I was left on the sidelines, so I spent the next few months trying to recover from a long, brutal, and financially draining political process. Not long after my campaign ended, I signed a book deal with Penguin Books, a contract with the Fox News Channel for a new television show, and a contract with the ABC Radio network to do daily commentaries. I was on the road just as much as, if not more than, I had been during the campaign, and I spent a lot of time campaigning for McCain and other Republican candidates all over the country. Just a few weeks before Christmas, I finished a grueling book tour that took me to fifty-three cities in eighteen days. I was exhausted physically, emotionally, and mentally. The time I spent in the Bahamas was a lifesaver. I don't think I even realized just how completely worn out I was until I finally had a chance to rest.

I took a nonstop JetBlue flight from Nassau to New York's JFK Airport, and when I got to the city, it was snowing, the temperature was in the twenties, and traffic was gridlocked as only New York traffic can be—a far cry from the beautiful, warm climate I'd left just a few hours earlier. I inched my way toward Midtown to start the preparation for a television show that would air the next day. My flight back home to North Little Rock was set for first thing Sunday morning. I hadn't been home in almost three weeks and was more than ready to sleep in my own bed and play with my three dogs, who I'm pretty sure had forgotten what I looked like.

The weather in New York was getting worse, and late Friday

afternoon, Delta Air Lines called to tell me that my flight for Sunday was already canceled. Because it was Christmas week, every other flight was booked solid until Tuesday, and even then they could only put me on standby. It was beginning to look like I might not make it home in time, and my hopes for a simple Christmas were beginning to die as things became more and more complicated.

Because I'm on planes four to five days a week, I have enough frequent flyer miles to qualify for the highest level of service on several airlines. This usually makes traveling a lot easier because I have a special phone number I can call for help, priority when booking and boarding, and usually the opportunity to upgrade to first class for no extra cost. But this weekend these advantages weren't helping me at all. I knew that the weather was better south of New York and if I could get to Washington, DC, I might be able to get a flight from there. I decided to take a train from New York's Penn Station to DC late Saturday night after I finished taping the show and then catch an early flight from DC to Arkansas on Sunday. There was space available on the train to DC, and Delta had a flight that would work, but the first two Delta agents I spoke to on the phone told me I couldn't change my ticket. I explained that I would pay for my ticket and lodging and that, by switching my flight, I would be doing them a favor because I'd be freeing up a seat on one of the flights out of New York. I figured this compromise was more than fair.

Somehow, neither of the first two people I spoke with saw it that way. They had "rules" and the "rules" wouldn't let me change the ticket. I asked for a supervisor; I got disconnected. I called back and had to explain my plan, which I thought was brilliant, all over again. I was more than ready to take my problem off their hands and had figured out how to do it at no cost to them! I realize that Christmas is one of the busiest travel seasons of the year and that, with passengers in a hurry to get to where they are going, the reservations and information people at the airlines are frazzled. I also know that my flight wasn't the only one canceled and that there were hundreds of people just like me who were upset and anxious. I know that. I understand that. But at the time, I didn't care about being logical or benignly accepting rational excuses. I wanted to *get home for Christmas*!

I can be a stubborn person when I want something badly enough. I kept calling the airline and finally talked to someone who seemed to understand that her job was not to read the rule book but to serve the people who paid her salary and help them solve their problems. That agent deserves a raise. Not only that, she should be promoted and put in charge of training other people. She approved the ticket change, I booked a train ticket and hotel room for DC, and despite the train's being an hour and a half late, I finally made it to DC around 1:00 A.M., snuck a brief nap before getting up at 4:00, went to Reagan National airport, and caught a flight to Arkansas that got me home in time for Christmas, even if it was several hours later than I had planned.

I felt like Steve Martin's character in the hilarious movie *Planes, Trains and Automobiles.* Add a boat to that equation, since I had had to take a boat from the island in the Bahamas where we stayed to Nassau before I flew to New York, and you can basically picture my experience. It took perseverance, patience, and persuasion to do it, but I got home. My eight days at home during Christmas were literally the longest stretch of time I had spent in my own home since my wife, Janet, and I had bought the place two years earlier.

When people asked me what I wanted for Christmas that year, my response was "I want to be home." I really meant it. There was no material thing that occupied my imagination and "want list" nearly as much as my simple desire to be home with my wife, kids, and dogs.

As I went through the logistical gymnastics of finding a way home, I was reminded of how absurd it seems to have to go through so much effort to do something so simple. I couldn't help but think of how complicated my life had become, with nonstop travel, hotel stays five or more nights a week, speaking engagements around the country, a weekly television show, a constant barrage of e-mails, and plans to do radio commentaries three times a day, five days a week. Don't misunderstand me—I'm truly grateful to be busy. It's an enormous blessing to have a job (several, actually!) and be able to pay my bills and expenses. Nonetheless, life is more complicated than I could ever have imagined it growing up in a working-class family in Arkansas. And I thought for Christmas I just wanted things to be *simple*. I wanted a simple Christmas.

I thought of the first Christmas and how Joseph and Mary had seen their plans to get home get all messed up as well. I'm sure they wanted to be back in Nazareth for the birth of their baby, but instead they ended up stuck in Bethlehem (though in their case, weather and airlines had nothing to do with it). They didn't realize it, but they were having an appointment with destiny. Centuries earlier, when the prophets had predicted the birth of the Messiah, the city for his arrival wasn't Nazareth or even Jerusalem. Instead, it was the sleepy little village of Bethlehem, and although neither Joseph nor Mary had any freinds there, it was inevitable that their baby would be born there. I'm sure they suffered some anxious moments trying to figure out what they would do if they didn't get home. After all, that's where their families were. That's where they would have support and comfort and be surrounded by those who could help make the birth as easy as possible. Instead, all of their hopes and prayers couldn't sway the will of God, who had determined long ago how His son would be brought into the world.

There are times in our lives when things go exactly according to plan. But when God has a bigger purpose than we can possibly imagine, none of our efforts—no matter how well intentioned or practical—will change the course he has set for us. We might be able to get Delta Air Lines to change our flight, but only God can control the actual journey, and no matter how strange or irrational it might seem to us, there is a purpose to the path.

I'm glad God didn't find a reason to keep me in New York for Christmas. Had He willed it, I would never have made it home. But luckily, my desire to get home didn't challenge an eternally prescribed destiny. My only obstacles were weather, airline schedules, and a couple of out-of-sorts reservation agents who just wanted their shifts to end. God orchestrated every moment of the first Christmas—at the dismay, I'm sure, of Joseph and Mary, who must have been frightened out of their wits—but in the end, he kept it simple. And that, I've learned, is the true message of Christmas—just keep it simple.

A Simple Christmas

Whenever I think about the Christmas story, I think about how, if I were God, I would have done the whole thing very differently. After all, the first Christmas was an incredibly big deal. God had decided to show up on earth in the form of a human being so He could show us once and for all how human life is supposed to be lived. For thousands of years, He had watched from heaven as humans destroyed what He had created so carefully. Being God, He knew this was going to happen, and sure enough, it did, but He had a plan.

He had sent prophets, given very explicit written instructions, and even blurted out some pretty loud pronouncements on top of mountains—sometimes with fire, other times with floods—but even though His voice was probably even louder than an Aerosmith concert, people kept being, well, people.

The very first Christmas was going to be a pretty big deal—God wouldn't just write a book or hold a news conference with a spokesman giving a briefing on the way things needed to be. He was coming in person, which in itself would be huge, since no one had ever actually seen God in person. He was always around, but He never showed up "with skin on" and start walking around like us. This time, He was going to take on the form of a human being and hang out in a body like ours and live in the world with us so He could give us the plan in person and live it out in front of us so we wouldn't be able to say we didn't understand. He wasn't going to just *tell* us what to do anymore; He was going to *show* us.

I know a little about promoting a big event. After all, I did run for president (unsuccessfully, but I still did okay given the budget I had to work with), I ran for governor a few times (successfully), and I have launched a TV show and a daily nationwide radio commentary, and been a best-selling author. Sure, it's a far cry from creating the universe, but I figure I have some insight into staging a big event.

And if I'd been God, this whole Christmas deal would have been handled differently.

We're talking about the biggest event since the Beatles on *Ed Sullivan,* Woodstock, or the inaugural events for my swearing in as president. (Okay, so Woodstock was a muddy mess with good music but not nearly enough porta-potties, and my presidential inauguration got derailed by some guy named Obama, but you get my point.)

But God showing up on earth in person? With a face we can see and voice we can hear—the whole deal? An event of this magnitude calls for pulling out all the stops. I'd hire the best caterers and some great bands, get the staging just right, and pick a venue that would be impossible for the press to ignore— maybe Times Square or the National Mall, or maybe really rattle the liberals and do the whole thing right in the middle of San Francisco! Of course, we'd do worldwide satellite feeds and set up remote viewing sites everywhere. There would be various levels of sponsorship, product placements, and of course, naming rights. It would make the Super Bowl look like a Little League game!

But God didn't do it anything like that. If I didn't know better, I'd think the way He showed up for the first Christmas was bungled badly by the worst combination of poor planning and failed execution ever. From the standpoint of putting on a big event, He did *everything* wrong.

The first Christmas was a simple one. So simple it had all the makings of a first-class disaster. It's a miracle it turned out well at all. In fact, that's the whole point. It really was, and remains, a miracle. In fact, it was the greatest miracle of all time. And it really was simple.

The Christmas story we're used to hearing is so clean and neat. We've grown up seeing the sanitized church version performed at annual pageants each December, in which choirs sing, children put on bathrobes and grab broom handles to be shepherds and wise men, and we see a beautiful production with stars in the sky, angels singing, and a quiet and clean little baby, who never even cries, resting peacefully in a box of hay. Judging from these nice little productions, one would think the Christmas story is a heart-warming, Oprah kind of tale, when the actual version probably resembled something closer to Jerry Springer!

I'm not being disrespectful toward the birth of God's son. In fact, as strange as it is, that's the way the whole thing was planned. When God decided to show up in person, He did it in a way that totally defied conventional wisdom. After all, He was the "King," and we are used to kings showing up wearing some fancy clothes and surrounded by an army, a band with lots of loud brass horns, and an enormous number of attendants to take care of everything from booking the hotels to tipping the baggage handlers to even tasting the food. But the scene of the original Christmas didn't follow this script—not even close.

The story starts with a fairly simple fourteen-year-old girl named Mary and a scraggly teenage boy named Joseph. Mary and Joseph led pretty quiet lives, and neither of them was all that big a deal in their little hometown of Nazareth, which itself was unimportant at that time.

Joseph was Mary's boyfriend. There was nothing unusual about a teenager having a boyfriend, but Mary also had a secret: She had a baby inside her, and she wouldn't be able to hide it much longer. It wasn't as common back then as it is now for a young, unwed girl to become a mother, but it wasn't unheard of. But Mary also had another secret that *was* unheard of. She adamantly insisted she had never had sex with anyone, including Joseph. That was hard for her parents, or anyone else, for that matter, to believe. The only person who believed Mary when she said she and Joseph had never slept together was Joseph himself. But he was still having a very hard time accepting the idea that Mary really hadn't been with anyone else. He wanted to believe she was telling the truth because he didn't want to have to confront the pain of knowing that the girl he hoped to marry one day had been unfaithful to him even before they had exchanged their vows.

Although there was speculation over who the father of Mary's child was, there was no doubt that this young girl was pregnant. It was humiliating to her and to her family to have people talk behind their backs and gossip about who had gotten Mary pregnant.

Mary and Joseph had discussed marriage, but now a baby would be involved from the beginning, and Joseph would have to accept that it wasn't his. What's worse, Mary not only was claiming that she hadn't been with another man but was actually insistent that an angel had come to her from heaven and announced that she would be having God's child. The young man demonstrated an amazing love for this girl, having to actually believe either that she was talking to angels and having God's child or that she was a very mentally disturbed person, but because he loved her so much he was willing to accept her delusional tendencies.

Several months into Mary's pregnancy, Joseph was summoned to the town of Bethlehem, where he had been born, to register for a census that King Herod wanted done. It was clearly a typical government deal—making the entire population travel back to the city of their birth rather than just sending a few census takers to the communities to ask the questions. I would be more critical of such an absurd policy, but today, two thousand years later, the government still does things that are just as inexplicable, like having elderly women take off their shoes and get virtually strip-searched at an airport before getting on a plane to go see their grandkids.

For Mary and Joseph, this meant a trip from Nazareth to Bethlehem; the two towns were about eighty miles apart, but the most popular route took a longer way bypassing Samaria, making it about a week's journey. This sort of trip—twenty miles or more a day on a donkey or walking over rugged and rocky terrain—was very dangerous for a pregnant girl, especially when there were no hospitals on the way. I'm sure this didn't help Joseph believe Mary's story that she was having God's child, because wouldn't God want to do everything possible to make sure that the mother of His child was safe and that His child would be born in a nice, clean, stable place? Instead, it was as if everything that could go wrong did: Young girl gets pregnant, can't really explain who the father is, and is forced to make a long journey with a teenage boy so he can carry out some idiotic government mandate. This was bad enough, but then, to add insult to injury, once the couple arrived at their destination, got counted by the government, and started to head back home, she went into labor.

It's not like there was a stretch of Marriotts along the freeway from Bethlehem to Nazareth. Of course, there were no freeways, either. Back then people would often rent out some space in their homes to be used as inns for travelers who needed a place to stay. But because of the census, there were more people traveling than usual, so all the extra rooms were filled. The couple was getting pretty desperate when a local resident, who felt sorry for these two young teenagers, offered to let them camp out in his barn for the night. The barn was nothing like the red wooden ones we see in the cornfields of Iowa today. In fact, it was actually a stone cave, since it was fairly typical in that day to use natural grottoes as shelters for animals.

Throughout history, this "innkeeper," as he has been described, has been vilified for "having no room in the inn" and forcing a frightened teenage mother to give birth to the son of God in such an uncomfortable, dirty place. But this is unfair to him. He couldn't give what he didn't have (a vacant room), but he gave what he did have and appears to have done so willingly and joyfully. We can't blame him for the lack of space, but we can certainly credit him for trying to make the best of a bad situation. At least he gave what he had; many of us have far more than an animal shelter but don't even offer that to God. We act with an air of indignation that we'd certainly make the comfort of Jesus a higher priority, but would we? Jesus has never expected us to give Him what we *wished* we had, but rather has always tested to see if we would simply give from what we *did* have.

Have you ever said, "If I had a million dollars, I'd give God half"? Get over it. God knows you don't have a million dollars, and if he really wanted you to have it, he'd probably give it to you. But you do have *something*—probably more than you think—so use what you *have*.

It's not known whether the innkeeper at the Bethlehem "Barnyard Inn" provided any assistance to the young couple other than the space, but it seems evident that, no matter what he did, it still wasn't the best of circumstances for a birth. Instead of a nice birthing room with soft music and sterile walls and floors, Joseph and Mary had a cave full of barnyard animals. Instead of nurses and doctors with pristine hospital gowns and masks, the most assistance the couple could've hoped to receive would've been from some local woman who might have overheard the screams of the scared teenage girl, and most likely the screams of her equally scared teenage boyfriend. Sheep, goats, and other livestock had probably been the only previous occupants of that little cave, and we can only imagine the odor and filth that likely greeted Jesus when He chose to arrive on earth as a human being for the first time. The anxiety of being away from her own mother and family would have been traumatic enough for Mary, but I can only imagine the sheer terror she felt as the intense pain of labor set in and she had no one nearby to offer Lamaze coaching, encouragement, or words of experience, much less a saddle block or an epidural.

We always see the sanitized version of the birth of Jesus, a bloodless, somber, and somewhat silent affair, as depicted in the various church Christmas cantatas or typified by the classic hymn "Silent Night." Silent night my foot! I'll bet that Mary and Joseph were both screaming and the baby was crying and the animals were all wound up as well. It may have been an "immaculate conception," but the notion that the birth was immaculate is definitely a stretch. It was the same bloody, yucky mess that marks any birth, except at this one there were no clean towels, sterilized clips to cut the umbilical cord, or incubator to place the child in to keep him warm. In fact, one thing we do know was that upon his birth, Jesus was "wrapped in swaddling clothes and laid in a manger." How precious!

Oh, really? Swaddling clothes are nothing more than rags that were tightly wrapped around a newborn to keep him warm, dry, and secure.

The "manger" was nowhere near as romantic as it sounds. It was simply a rough wood water or feed trough for the animals. Not long before the son of God was placed in it, livestock had eaten grain out of it. God spent His first few moments as a human in a food dish.

From our perspective this sounds like a plan gone bust. But it wasn't a plan gone bust. It was *the* plan from the beginning. God had no intention of opening the sky and landing like a little Superman from a faraway planet. He didn't plot an arrival that was all about huge ceremonies and fine linens, festive music, scrubby-clean surroundings, and the latest advancements in medical technology. From the beginning, God wanted to show up in the lowliest of conditions so that in the future, no one would assume that their own situation was simply too humble as to merit His attention. However low people might feel, God wanted to demonstrate that He'd "been there, done that." His first bed was an animal's food dish, His first outfit was some dirty old rags, and His first roommates were cows and sheep. Top that, whiners of the world!

I once heard a Christmas sermon by a minister who seemed to get the real picture. The sermon was called "Making Love on a Dirty Street." Sure grabs your attention, huh? The title might be a bit risqué for some tastes, but it pretty well makes it clear that the greatest act of God's love happened in the least likely of places, and it reminds us that if God can show up for his own arrival on earth in a place like that, then He can show up wherever we are, no matter how dirty, dangerous, or humble it may be.

It's an expression not of humility but of arrogance to say, "God wouldn't understand how low I feel or how horrible my situation is." If anything, most of us can't ever imagine just how low and horrible *His* situation started out to be. Next time you start to think you have it really bad, take some comfort in knowing that God understands exactly how you feel.

That's the *real* Christmas story. It wasn't pretty and pristine but dark and dirty. It was a humiliating experience for the young lady who had to become a woman the night she gave birth to God's own son. She probably wondered why the Creator of the universe didn't provide a better staging area for his arrival, but the nice stages, melodious music, and fancy costumes would have to wait a few centuries until churches came along and added them to the picture. But who can blame the church for coming up with an inaccurate version of the story? The real version seemed so unlikely and so hard to explain and defend that it's easier to tell the modern version. Oh, sure, some shepherds eventually showed up, but wouldn't you think that the birth of the son of God would warrant a visit from the mayor or at least a letter from the chamber of commerce? Instead, Jesus was welcomed into the world by some young boys herding sheep in the middle of the night who dropped by the cave full of cows to say, "Hey, God, glad you came."

We're used to Christmas being a time of comfort, celebration, and good times. We exchange gifts with our friends and family, dine on a feast in a nice, warm home, and maybe relax by a warm fire as we sip hot cocoa. We dress up in nice clothes and go to church to light candles, sing pretty songs, and bow our heads in reverence to the birth of God's son. We fuss for weeks in advance to make sure everything is just right—the gifts are perfect, the decorations are hung, and the Christmas ham is juicy and delicious. If something doesn't go according to our plan, we think Christmas will be ruined, but we forget the real story of that first Christmas. It's hard to think that the Nativity could have been so dirty and dangerous when we're sitting in a quiet church or nestled in warm sweaters by the Christmas tree, but if we take time to think about the first Christmas the way it *really* was, we might better appreciate all the things God has blessed us with a bit more.

This book is a collection of Christmas stories from my past that have taught me valuable lessons about what Christmas is really all about. Many of them are funny. Some of them are sad. I hope you enjoy reading them, but I also hope that you take some time to reflect on the first Christmas and that you remember how simple that first Christmas really was.

A Simple Christmas

1.

Patience

"You'll just have to wait until Christmas!"

I heard that a lot during my childhood and never liked it. Even though we spend weeks preparing for Christmas, all of the anticipation and excitement is focused on December 25. Until then, we are required to stare longingly at all of the nicely wrapped boxes with our names on them sitting under the tree and wonder what fantastic gift is waiting for us—so close yet so far. I've never understood the point in waiting until a particular day to get a perfectly good gift that has, obviously, already been purchased and is intended specifically for you. Why not just let the person get as much enjoyment out of it as possible and give it to them right away?

In most areas of my life, I have matured and seasoned with age, but I have never outgrown my impatience, and I still don't understand this idea of "waiting until Christmas." Anything as wonderful as Christmas surely ought to be celebrated and observed as soon as possible, right?

I've never been a patient man. I've asked God to grant me patience, but my prayer usually goes something like, "Lord, give me patience and give it to me *right now*!" I've never understood why I should have to wait to get something tomorrow if it's possible to get it today. I love jet aircraft, microwave ovens, shopping online twenty-four hours a day, and overnight shipping. If Fred Smith hadn't beaten me to it, I'm pretty sure I would have invented Federal Express just so I could get my stuff quicker.

I don't stand in line for anything that isn't absolutely necessary—even at the airport. I was one of the early sign-ups to pay extra for a "Fly CLEAR" card, which allowed me, for an annual fee, to get a background check, fingerprints and an iris scan, and a biometric ID. I still had to go through security, mind you (the whole thing with shoes off, junk out of pockets, laptop in the plastic washtub, etc.), but the CLEAR card saved me time, and that was helpful on the days when I was really pushing it to catch my plane on time (especially since I'm sure as heck not important enough for an airline to hold a plane for me). Sure it's extra money, and some people might think it's unnecessary, but to me, it's worth every penny. Sadly, CLEAR abruptly went out of business in the summer of 2009. I guess not many people were as impatient as me.

I hate lines so much that I've missed eating at great restaurants, going to a lot of movies and concerts, and meeting famous and important people because it involved standing in line. Take my word for it, if you see me standing in a long line, it's either because there's something I *have* to do, there's something I want to do *very* intensely (not likely), or (more likely) my wife is with me and *she* thinks it's worth the wait.

My impatience is the stuff of legend with my kids. They love regaling their friends with stories of my obsession with not wasting time in a line or waiting for a "special day" like Father's Day or my birthday to get something I want. They dread buying me Christmas presents because they know that if I tell them I want something, I'm likely to just buy it for myself before they can get it, wrap it, and put it under the tree.

When my kids were little, my wife, Janet, and I saved money for two years for a trip to Disney World. I had heard Disney sometimes has long lines at peak season, so I did my usual thorough research. I bought both the official and unofficial guidebooks to the parks, and I actually found out which month and which days of that month had the lowest number of visitors and planned our trip during those days. I plotted our every move—what time to enter the park, which entrance to go through, and which rides would be most efficient to ride and in what order. I was as much a drill sergeant during this trip as I was a dad, but by gosh, we stayed on schedule!

The whole time, my kids rolled their eyes and made fun of me, but we never waited in line longer than a minute or two, and we rode every ride and saw every attraction in the Magic Kingdom, MGM, and Epcot. My kids' friends told stories of how when they went to Disney, they only got to ride some of the amusements because they stood in line so long and missed things they wanted to do. My kids might have laughed at their obsessed father and his printed schedule, but they didn't miss a thing! In fact, they even got to ride some of the really cool rides several times.

On another occasion, when I took them to Israel, they called it the Today I Ran Where Jesus Walked Tour in recognition of the brisk pace at which we sprinted around the majestic land of the Bible. I do think that if Moses had had me along for the journey to the Promised Land, we could have shaved off a few of those forty years wandering around in the desert.

Most kids get excited around Christmastime, especially in the run-up to opening presents, but I was especially eager (and, admittedly, still am). I know that patience is supposed to be a virtue and all that, but I never could see anything all that virtuous about knowing darn well what I wanted and having to be tortured by the fact that even though it had already been purchased, wrapped, and placed under the tree, I had to wait until December 25 to actually get to use it. Made no sense to me. So I decided to beat the system.

My parents both worked, and my sister, Pat, and I used to stay with my grandparents, who lived across the street, during the day until either our mom or our dad got home. As we got a bit older, we started staying at our house by ourselves. In those days, it was pretty safe for parents to leave their kids at home alone, since there wasn't much crime and no one even bothered to lock their doors. There was no Internet, so our parents didn't have to worry that we were browsing pornography sites, and since our only TV was a black-and-white Philco that took several minutes to warm up and only received three channels originating from Shreveport, Louisiana, there was no danger of us watching any inappropriate television. Other than Popeye cartoons and *The Three Stooges,* there wasn't much that interested us on TV anyway, and it was easier and more fun to just join all the other neighborhood kids for pretty much unrestricted romping through the neighborhood until it got too dark or we got too hungry to stay outside.

As Christmas approached and boxes began appearing under the tree with my name on them, I became convinced that it was absurd to let good days of play go to waste, so I convinced Pat, who is two years older than me, that we should make sure that the packages contained the things we wanted and that taking the time to inspect them before Christmas would ensure that all the gifts were in good working order and not damaged in shipping. For whatever reason, it seemed logical to her, and so we began our annual secret Christmas tradition of what I like to call the "real twelve days of Christmas."

Pat was not only more patient than I was but also quite skillful at unwrapping the gifts, carefully sliding the gift wrap from the boxes, and then very artfully rewrapping them so that all of the loot was back under the tree, just as it had been, before our parents got home. Pat was a theater and English major in college and later taught acting and theater at the high-school level for many years, but I don't think she gave me proper credit for helping to launch her career by giving her the opportunity to hone her acting chops by explaining to our parents how anxious we were to know what was in our Christmas packages and asking if they would please tell us or let us open something early. Her talent for feigning total ignorance of what we'd be getting for Christmas in the days running up to the big moment was brilliant, but Christmas morning was truly an Oscar-worthy performance as she shrieked with glee and acted flabbergasted as she opened her boxes and convinced everyone in the room that she was absolutely surprised to behold these fine gifts. Heck, she had me believing that she was surprised, and I knew darn well that she had already had that thing out of the box every day for the past two weeks!

I also did my best to convey surprise as I opened my gifts. Phrases like "Wow! I can't believe it!" freely burst from my mouth when the only thing that would have surprised me was if, somehow, I had gotten anything other than whatever toy I held in my hands. My parents beamed as they watched my sister and me scream with delight and awe and undoubtedly congratulated themselves for their brilliant gift selection and for doing such a fine job of creating just the right magic of Christmas suspense.

Sometimes, my parents got us gifts that were too large to be wrapped and placed under the tree, but that didn't pose any problem for us. We got pretty good at combing every possible hiding place that might exist in our house, and few items escaped our detective work. It's too bad that we weren't assigned the task of locating the body of Jimmy Hoffa when the longtime labor boss disappeared. I'm pretty sure we could have found him in short order.

We didn't keep a record of just how many years this whole Christmas-morning-surprise business continued, since we didn't want to leave any records of the crime. We were practicing plausible deniability long before we knew what that meant or how it could be used in a cover-up. It's fair to say that most of our early Christmas experiences were filled with joy on two fronts—

joy that we got something, and greater joy for having enjoyed our gifts and not gotten caught, even though we had already worn some of them out long before their official unveiling.

It's a well-known fact that most criminals get sloppy once they become successful, and while I'm not sure that what we did was an actual crime, I have chosen not to reveal these stories until now, when I am sure the statute of limitations has long since passed on any punishment my parents could dole out. Until now, I was certain that, if they found out what my sister and I had been up to, they would cut us out of the will.

Even though we weren't criminals, our "crime" did become sloppier as time went on. Our ruse came to a crashing halt one particularly careless Christmas when I was about nine or ten during which I got sloppy in more ways than one. My requested gift that year was a new football. Like most of what we received at Christmas, it would be ordered from one of three Christmas catalogs that came to our house—Sears, Montgomery Ward, and J. C. Penney.

After school, football fairly well dominated the afternoons for the kids of our neighborhood during the fall football season. We'd gather on the vacant field behind my grandparents' house and play until it was so dark that the football hit us in the face because we couldn't see it anymore.

My parents bought me my requested gift that year—a brown leather J.C. Higgins football from Sears. It was a nice ball, and I was excited to use it. My friends and I always hoped that at least one of us got a new football each year, because it usually took us about that long to wear the old one out. This was the first year that I was getting the football, and given that it was my first really official, regulation-sized, leather football, I was pretty proud of it and could hardly be expected to wait until Christmas Day to play with it. Heck, the season would end pretty soon after that, and I couldn't think of any reason to miss out on a couple of prime weeks to enjoy such a great gift.

Each day, Pat and I would hurry home from school and she would go to work like a skillful surgeon removing the tape and paper, and we'd spend the afternoon playing with our new stuff until it was time to put everything back where we'd gotten it before our parents got home.

The year I got my football, I was so excited to use it that I guess one day our game ran a little late and I wasn't as careful as I should have been when I had to put the ball away. I just knew that when I opened my presents on Christmas Day and tore into the box with the football, all my now keenly developed acting skills would never mask the fact that my "brand new" football was covered in mud! I suggested that maybe it was a new marketing ploy by Sears to create a greater sense of reality by shipping the football with mud and dirt already on it. I admit that it was a pretty lame explanation, but I didn't have much to work with. With suspicions now aroused, further examination of our Christmas loot revealed a chemistry set with half the experiments already done and a doll with batteries not included that somehow had mysteriously been blessed with new batteries.

The jig was up. We almost had our gifts that year confiscated and sent to some kids in China. My parents had always told me, "Eat every bite of food on that plate! There are kids in China who would be glad to have it, so you aren't going to waste it," and as disappointed as I was at the prospect of having my gifts sent halfway around the world, I figured it was only fair that some little Chinese boy get my football, since I'd been eating his food for years. I wasn't sure if he would even understand football, but I had learned my lesson! At any rate, my parents finally cooled off before they actually sent the toys to Shanghai. I actually think they thought it was kind of funny and even admired how incredibly resourceful Pat and I had turned out to be. I think they figured that with gall like that, we'd end up either running the country or in jail. Luckily, I've ended up closer to the former than the latter, and since I've since stopped unwrapping my Christmas gifts early, I hope it will stay that way.

I have to confess that, although I don't sneak open my presents anymore, I haven't really changed much. I still want to open stuff once it's under the tree. I figure there's stuff there I might enjoy now, and if a truck were to run me over before Christmas Day, I'd never even know what I got, never would have the pleasure of using it, and wouldn't have the opportunity to thank the person who got it for me. For years my wife has hidden presents so I couldn't shake the boxes or worse, open and reseal them. (She's heard the stories.) Of course, she hides things so well that every year, there are at least a couple of presents that she can't find again. Some Christmas items don't arrive until March or April when she accidently stumbles across long-lost and virtually forgotten Christmas packages. This only validates my still-strong view that we should give the gifts upon purchase to avoid such embarrassing moments as having hidden the presents so well that a team from CSI has to come in and help find them.

I admit that I'm a bit obsessive on the patience at Christmas issue, but most everyone wants Christmas to come sooner rather than later. I'll admit that maybe my eagerness for presents is a bit extreme, and I'll admit that some things are worth the wait (at least having to wait to get that brand-new toy or gadget makes it even more exciting when you actually *do* get it), but Christmas is not just about the gifts, the food, and the decorations. I think the excitement over Christmas comes from a longing in the human spirit to know if there really is a God and, if there is, to get together with him right away. For hundreds of years before the birth of Jesus, the prophets were telling everyone to get ready because He was coming. They thought it would be soon, though it didn't seem to be happening on their timetable.

When it did happen, it really snuck up on just about everyone. God obviously didn't want the kind of manufactured joy and superficial "frou-frou" that would have inevitably surrounded a highly publicized entrance on the planet. He kept things simple. And He kept us waiting and never caved in to the impatience, even the petulance, of the prophets and priests who thought His coming would bring glory to them. After all, wouldn't it be worth the wait? If everlasting life isn't worth waiting for, then what is?! By the time Jesus really did show up in Bethlehem, some of the most religious people and the high religious leaders had things all planned for His arrival, and they were pretty much in the center of the whole show. That's one of the reasons they didn't recognize the event when it did happen. The elaborate and opulent entrance that they envisioned never took place. No palace, but instead a little cave full of farm animals. There weren't fine linens and silks like they had prepared, just some strips of worn cloth that were used to wrap up the little baby.

This to me sounds like the perfect Christmas. I don't mean the dangerous labor that the young Mary had to go through or the fear she and Joseph must have felt knowing they were all alone in the desert with no one to help them deliver this child into the world. I mean the lack of pomp and wrapping. I never have liked all that wrapping, and I've spent my life wanting to take the wrapping off the things people give me. I just can't wait. I believe that gifts should be given in a spirit of goodwill, not a spirit of "You can't have it until the day you're *supposed* to have it." Maybe it's a character flaw, but I like to think of it as part of my spiritual DNA. I really believe that the arrival of Jesus on earth is such a big deal that I can't wait to find out about it. I'm ready to unwrap Him and get Him moving around and doing big things. I can't see a reason to keep Him hidden from everybody. A lot of people need Him now. This is the true meaning of Christmas. The presents are just something extra, and couldn't it be argued that making people wait until Christmas to open their much-anticipated gifts takes the attention away from what Christmas is really all about? I think that's a pretty good argument, don't you?

I know I need to be more patient about some things in life—I really do. Maybe this year I'll make a concerted effort to not shake the boxes under the tree, and maybe if I ask for something, I'll actually let one of my kids buy it for me. (Though considering I'm pretty set in my ways, that's pretty unlikely.) But footballs and chemistry sets aside, I still don't believe that we need to wait for some "special day" to find the real meaning of Christmas.

Yes, I've come to terms with my "sins" of unwrapping gifts before Christmas as a child and scheming to open them early even as an adult. And I've also come to realize that anticipation helps you appreciate things more. I could eat a green tomato and be fine, but allowing it to ripen to a bright red will give it the full flavor God intended it to have. I have learned that a carefully aged steak will have a full-bodied flavor that far surpasses that of cheaper cuts of meat. And I also know that the lifetime I spend on this broken earth filled with all of its shortcomings and problems and pressures will help me appreciate Heaven that much more when I finally get there.

There are some things in life that are best when experienced in their proper season and at the appropriate moment. It was a hard lesson for me to accept when I was a kid who just couldn't wait to get my new football, but I get it now. So what if it took me fifty years to figure it out?

I've also learned that even though presents are great, the greatest gift of all is the one God gave us that very first Christmas. He gave us the gift of life and of His love. Luckily, that's not something we have to wait for anymore!

2.

Sacrifice

On February 9, 1964, I was one of seventy-three million Americans watching *The Ed Sullivan Show* when the Beatles made their first appearance in the United States. My family usually watched *Ed Sullivan* anyway, but that night was something special.

Like many kids who saw this quartet of long-haired Brits with electric guitars and drums, I realized their music was something very different, and I immediately knew that I wanted a guitar so I could become one of the Beatles. So what if I was only eight years old at the time and had never played a guitar in my life? I wasn't concerned with minor details like that, and playing a guitar real loud and having girls scream for me seemed like a great goal in life. I was hooked.

The kids in my neighborhood were just as stricken as I was, and we started gathering Coke bottles that we found discarded on the side of the road and turning them in for their two-cent deposit value. Eventually we earned enough to buy the 45 rpm record of "I Want to Hold Your Hand," with "I Saw Her Standing There" on the B side of the record. It was the first record I ever bought. Before that, I only had little 78 rpm recordings of children's stories with songs, like "The Poky Little Puppy" and "Goldilocks and the Three Bears." Coke bottles (in the South, we call all soda Coke even if it's actually a different brand) were the great equalizer of economic disparity among kids where I came from. Some kids automatically got money from their parents as an allowance, which seemed pretty terrific, but the rest of us could take our little red wagons (everyone had one) and pull them around town and pick up enough empty bottles to get some easy money, even if it did require some serious scavenging around tall weeds and ditches.

The little record player I had was better suited for "Poky Little Puppy" records, but it would play a 45, although I had to turn the volume all the way up to get anywhere near the "rock and roll" level I wanted. The little two-inch speaker distorted horribly when pushed up to ten on the dial, but I didn't care. The louder the better. Unfortunately, the louder-the-better mind-set stayed with me after I advanced to larger speakers backed up by an amplifier that emitted 120 decibels—enough to take paint off the wall! Yes, I know that I shouldn't have played music that loudly, and yes, it has affected my hearing somewhat, and yes, I regret it. I have already had the lectures from my parents when I was a kid and from doctors as an adult, so please spare me another one!

Playing the 45s and later the LP albums of the Beatles was

great, but that really wasn't enough to fulfill my passion for rock and roll. That summer, several kids in the neighborhood decided we would produce a Beatles show for our parents and all the neighbors. Of course, we didn't have real instruments and none of us knew how to play, but those were minor details. We would make our own instruments and pantomime the songs played by the record player.

Every kid in the neighborhood had a job. My sister Pat ran the record player. Amelia Leverett from down the street sold tickets and Cokes. The "Beatles" consisted of Tom Frazier as George Harrison (he would later give up being a Beatle to become a prominent hand surgeon); Carol Frazier (Tom's sister, who is now married and works as a community-affairs specialist at a pediatric hospital) as Ringo; Betty Rodden (who, last I heard, was a basketball coach) as John Lennon; and me as Paul McCartney, the bass player (I'm still one today). Bob "Bo" Frazier, the little brother of Tom and Carol (now a CPA), was the opening act and entertained the audience by wearing a bedsheet and singing a song called "Ghostly Solo." It had absolutely nothing to do with the Beatles, but Mr. and Mrs. Frazier wouldn't let us use their back patio as a stage unless we included Bo in the show.

Our guitars were cardboard cutouts taped and glued to yardsticks, and the drums were made from round patio tables turned upside down. The larger tables were used for the bass drums, and the smaller tables were for the other drums. Cymbals were cardboard cutouts attached to mop handles.

Our families and the other neighbors were quite charitable and paid twenty-five cents each for a ticket to watch us lip-synch as many Beatles records as we had been able to purchase with the money earned from collecting Coke bottles. I'm sure they were all glad we hadn't found more bottles!

The Fraziers were better off than most of us in the neighborhood and owned an 8 mm movie camera. Somewhere the movies that were made of this momentous event probably still exist, but I pray daily that no amount of coercion ever forces anyone to cough them up for public consumption.

Playacting the Beatles with cardboard and yardsticks was okay, but I wanted a real guitar. It shouldn't have surprised anyone who knew me back then. As young as age five, I was banging away at an old Gene Autry cowboy guitar that my dad had and would play occasionally. At the time, I thought I was Elvis or at least figured I would replace him as soon as I got old enough or he retired. (The photo on the cover of this book is in fact one of me at five years old with that old Gene Autry guitar, striking my best Elvis pose.)

Most of the other kids in our "band" moved on to other things after that night on the "stage." Not me. I was hooked, but I didn't want to spend the rest of my life lip-synching songs with a cardboard guitar (Milli Vanilli would do that just fine several years later). I wanted to "do the *real* thing." (Sounds almost like a book I think you ought to read called *Do the Right Thing*.)

I decided I wanted an electric guitar. I asked for but didn't get one for Christmas of 1964. Ditto for 1965. By 1966, when I was the ripe old age of eleven, I decided that I had to change my strategy. Each year until then, I had made a Christmas list of things I wanted. I knew the list had a lot more on it than could ever be expected, but I wanted to cover all the bases. As I "matured," and got wiser, it occurred to me that while I had included the electric guitar on the list, there were other things on that list as well, and I was in effect giving my parents a way out of giving me an electric guitar, which was all I really wanted anyway.

In 1966, my Christmas list was very simple. An electric guitar. That's it. The whole list. Nothing else on it. No more negotiating and compromising. It was all or nothing.

They said, "Son, don't you want to put something else on that list in case Santa can't come up with a guitar?" Not that I still believed in Santa or anything, but heck no, I didn't want to put something else on that list! Been there, done that, and still no guitar. I dug in my heels.

"All I want is the guitar. Nothing else," I told them. "I promise I'll practice and learn how to play it. If I don't, you can take it away from me." Of course, I knew that if I ever really got that guitar, I would practice it. and anyone taking it away was probably as likely as someone going up to Chuck Norris and taking away his chest hair. Ain't happening.

Of course, I had no idea what my parents could actually afford to buy me. I certainly was old enough and observant enough to know that we always drove a used car, didn't have air-conditioning like some families, never went on nice vacations like the Fraziers, and didn't get Eskimo Pies anytime we wanted like Amelia Leverett. But it never really occurred to me that we were that much different. I never asked to see my parents' checkbook or examine their tax returns to better assess their financial capacity. That stuff wasn't my problem anyway. I was concerned with one thing—getting that electric guitar.

I found one that seemed perfect in the J. C. Penney Christmas catalog. It was a red and black model with a white pick guard, and it came complete with a little amp, a carrying case, and an instruction book. The whole package was featured in the catalog at the special low price of ninety-nine dollars. I cut out the page and attached it to the piece of paper on which I had written my Christmas "list."

My parents asked me several times if I wouldn't mind giving them some "other ideas." I knew what that meant—"You aren't getting the guitar."

"Nothing doing!" I said. "You guys asked me what I wanted, and this is it. I want this or nothing." I was fully prepared to get nothing, and only years later did I find out how close I came to getting just that.

Was I being totally unreasonable, selfish, and ungrateful? Absolutely. But I honestly didn't realize it. At eleven, I really didn't know what my parents could or couldn't afford, and they hadn't asked me what I wanted *within their budget.* They had just asked what I wanted. Of course, through the years I asked for stuff I knew I wasn't going to get, like a pony, a chimpanzee, and a trip to Disneyland, but the guitar wouldn't poop all over the floor like a chimp, so I thought it might be a realistic request. And I really, truly wanted it.

Because of my previously confessed habit of opening up my gifts before Christmas, my parents had resorted to hiding things in places where I couldn't find them—apparently at the homes of people they worked with or at the fire station where my dad worked as a fireman. I guess they figured my sister and I couldn't go rummaging around places like that.

So as we gathered for the ritual of Christmas gift opening (which we did on the night of Christmas Eve most years because my dad usually worked on Christmas Day), nothing was under the tree for me. I had rolled the dice and gone for broke, and it was looking like I had crapped out. Nothing. Nada. I had said, "If I can't have the electric guitar, I don't want anything." For once, it looked like I was going to get exactly what I had asked for and most certainly what I deserved. My sister was all too happy about the entire thing—she was tearing into her stuff and holding each gift up and waving it about as if to say to me, "Sucker! You got nothing."

While I tried to do as my dad often told me and "take it like a man" (which translated to "Don't cry like a little girl"), I fought back tears and thought I was the biggest idiot in America for being so stubborn and not giving my parents any other options on my Christmas list.

After I had been made to feel thoroughly miserable at my situation, my dad excused himself from the gift giving and returned with a box. "Oh, I almost forgot that I have this one last thing for you," he said. The box didn't look like it would hold a pony or a chimpanzee, and I had no idea what it could be. Getting anything was somewhat comforting, just knowing that at least I was still considered family and wouldn't be sold into slavery or shipped off to China.

The box didn't look like a guitar, unless it was a guitar that was square and about eighteen inches high. I took it, opened it, and was truly bewildered. It was a small amplifier that looked very much like the one from the J. C. Penney Christmas catalog. But what a cruel joke—buy me an amplifier, but no guitar!

As I was opening the box, my mother had quietly slipped out of the room, and as I examined the amplifier, she returned and said, "You might find this to be useful to go with that." I looked up and saw that she held in her hand that very red and black electric guitar whose image I had memorized from staring at its picture in the catalog.

Move over Paul McCartney, Keith Richards, and Eric Clapton! Mike Huckabee has a guitar now! For all the taunting my sister had given me, this was the "game over" moment in my mind. It turned out she was actually excited for me and had known all along what my parents were up to but, amazingly, had kept it secret. (Remember, she became an acting teacher!) The taunting she had put me through earlier as she unwrapped her stuff was all part of the conspiracy that my family had contrived to make me truly think that I was about to have the lousiest Christmas a kid could have. It's a good thing that I didn't get anything else that year, because it would have been ignored anyway. I don't think that guitar left my hands for hours or even minutes. I held it and looked over every inch of it, carefully inspecting what I had only seen in the catalog picture before. The catalog hadn't done it justice. It was far more beautiful in person. I even held it in front of a mirror to see how I looked as a young rock star. Unquestionably, I looked like a complete dork, but at the time I thought I was the coolest kid around. (This was before I got glasses.)

Over the coming weeks, months, and years, I would play that guitar for hours. In those early weeks, when my fingers were not yet used to pushing the thin strings hard against the fret board, I played until my fingertips almost bled. I think even my parents were impressed—not that I was playing well, but that I truly was spending the hours practicing as I had promised.

That guitar my parents bought from J. C. Penney's Christmas catalog was more than just a Christmas gift; it was a key that unlocked many doors for me through the years. Believe it or not, I was actually a very shy person, and the thought of being in front of people was terrifying to me. Once I started playing, of course, I wanted to form a band. In the sixth grade, a few of my classmates and I formed a band. In the seventh grade, we played in public for the first time and performed what was surely a very powerful rendition of Wilson Pickett's "Midnight Hour." I'm sure there were maybe two hundred people in the audience, but it might as well have been Shea Stadium as far as I was concerned. As frightened as I was of a crowd, my desire to play music trumped any fear I had about being onstage. Somehow, I realized that I couldn't be a rock star and remain a recluse. Music did more than help me break out of my bashfulness. Unconsciously, music taught me teamwork, discipline, perseverance, and patience. I learned how to persevere through all of those hours of hard practice, and I came to understand what every musician knows—that for every minute onstage, there are *hours* of lonely practice that no one sees or appreciates. That is a lesson that served me well in speaking, writing, and every endeavor of which I've since been a part.

I played in several local rock and country bands through high school. I mostly played bass (an instrument that I would take up at age twelve because it became apparent that a lot more guys were playing guitar than bass, and if I learned bass, I figured my chances to be in a band were better). I also played drums for a while, but the guitar was my first and greatest love when it came to music.

A few years later, after I got married and found out that my wife, Janet, was pregnant with our first child, I was forced to make a very tough decision. Janet and I were hanging on by a thin thread financially, since I was trying to go to graduate school and work part time. Paying our rent each month was a challenge. We paid things on time, but only by being disgustingly frugal and never going into debt. When John Mark, our first son, was born, Janet had to quit her job to take care of him, and we were forced to take things day by day just to keep food in the house. The only things of value we had were my two guitars and the two amplifiers that powered them. I had been able to trade up through the years thanks to working at the local radio station and getting a few bucks from time to time for playing gigs, and now I owned a 1967 Gretsch Tennessean and a 1968 Fender Jazz Bass. They were valuable then, but years later they would have been worth enough to send my son to college. But at that moment in 1976, we were just trying to feed the boy and would worry about college later.

There was really only one option—I needed to sell the guitars. I put an ad in the local free "shopper" paper in Fort Worth, Texas, where we lived at the time. Calls came immediately for both, and within days, I found myself without any guitars for the first time since I was eleven. I cannot describe the pain of seeing someone gather up my prized equipment and take it away. I didn't ever let on to Janet how much it hurt letting go of those guitars; I knew that my priority was taking care of my family, and I never looked back, knowing I had made the right decision. A few years later, I was able to buy an old Yamaha acoustic at a pawnshop and would pick around on it and play it at church youth camp occasionally, but I knew that one day I'd like to have a bass guitar like the one I'd once had. Exactly twenty years later, Janet called me one day while I was in my office at the Capitol. I had been governor only a few weeks, and Janet and I were settling into the Governor's Mansion. She said she had been driving down the street and seen a bass that looked a lot like my old one, just a different color. She had gone in to ask about it and was calling to see if I thought it might be a good deal. She told me the year model—a 1967 Fender Jazz Bass. When she told me the asking price, I was sure she was mistaken. She repeated it to me. That's when I said, "Go back in there and write them a check for that amount and get out of there before they realize what that guitar could be worth." I was back in the bass business!

There were others on my staff at the Capitol who played instruments, and for the fun of it, we would gather in the basement of the Governor's Mansion to have jam sessions and blow off steam with music. We played a couple of songs for our staff at the 1996 Christmas party, and the fact that no one threw food at us was all the encouragement we needed. Capitol Offense, the band I still play in today, was born! The band developed, changed some personnel from time to time, but became fairly proficient, and over the years we played as an opening act for Willie Nelson, Grand Funk Railroad, the Charlie Daniels Band, Dionne Warwick, Percy Sledge, and 38 Special just to name a few. We played at two presidential inaugurations, two Republican National Conventions, and such venues as House of Blues in New Orleans and Red Rocks Amphitheatre in Denver. I'm often asked if we were that good, and I answer honestly that we didn't have to be—we were the only band in America that was fronted by a sitting governor, so we got some nice gigs!

In 2008, when I started my show on the Fox News Channel, I wanted to make homegrown music a part of it, using amateur, behind-the-scenes workers at the channel whose day jobs were in lighting, graphics, videography, engineering, and writing, but who, like me, had never given up the dream or the joy of playing. The music segment of our show is almost always the highest-rated segment and the audience favorite. Legendary artists like Willie Nelson, Ray Price, James Burton, Neil Sedaka, and Dion are just a few of the guests who have played with the Fox News Channel house band, the Little Rockers. Country greats like Aaron Tippin, Neal McCoy, Tracy Lawrence, Collin Raye, Clay Walker, the Bellamy Brothers, and many others have come on the show to share the stage with amateurs like us.

But if it hadn't been for my parents giving in to the demand of my stubborn eleven-year-old self and buying me that guitar for Christmas, none of this would have happened. Without that guitar, I probably never would have gained the confidence to be onstage and make speeches and run for office, and I certainly never would have gained the valuable tools of discipline, practice, and performance that music has taught me.

The real heroes of this story are Dorsey and Mae Huckabee, my hardworking and loving parents, who really did want to make my dream come true but weren't sure how they could do it.

I didn't know until years later, after I had kids of my own, just how much money ninety-nine dollars was to my parents back in 1966. It was *a lot* of money and a lot of money that they didn't have. They could have and should have told me no, but they gave up having a Christmas for themselves and bought me the guitar for which I had begged and pleaded for so long. They couldn't pay the ninety-nine dollars all at once, so they arranged to make monthly payments to J. C. Penney for a little over a year until they paid it off.

I wanted a simple Christmas that year. I didn't ask for a lot of things—just one that meant more to me than anything else I had ever asked for. But what was simple to me was anything but simple to my parents, who had to make a really major sacrifice to give it to me. The best Christmas gifts we get are the ones that represent a sacrifice on the part of the giver. That's because nothing so reflects what Christmas is all about as does sacrifice. God, who owed us nothing, gave us everything. He gave up more than His comfort and His crown—He gave His life, and it all started right there in a simple manger in Bethlehem.

It took years before the depth of my parents' sacrifice really sank in. By then, they were both gone. While they surely had some satisfaction in seeing me play onstage as a teenager and were comforted that as long as the noise of the guitar rang through our little house, they knew where I was, they probably never knew the impact that ninety-nine-dollar guitar had on me. I want to believe that if heaven is a place where all the good things are remembered and the bad things are forgotten, my parents are allowed to watch my show each week and see me playing music with not only my musical idols but theirs as well. They might actually believe that ninety-nine-dollar investment paid off!

Every Christmas, I still think about that guitar and the sacrifice that it represented. And I hope I don't forget to think about the greatest sacrifice of all, God's gift of Himself . . . a simple gift. After all, it was a simple Christmas.

P.S. I'll bet you're wondering whatever happened to the guitar from J. C. Penney. After a few years, I wanted to upgrade to a better guitar and sold it to a gentleman named Norman Gilbey in my hometown of Hope, Arkansas, for fifty dollars. In 1998, thirty years later, Capitol Offense was playing at the annual Watermelon Festival in Hope. Norman was there and came up to me and said, "You remember the guitar you sold me?"

"I sure do! Whatever happened to it? I later regretted selling it," I remarked.

"I still have it. It's been sitting in a closet most of these years. I didn't get to play it that much, so it's still in good shape," Norman revealed. He then asked if I'd like it back. I told him that he could name his price—I would love to have that first guitar back. He argued with me about payment and insisted that I just take it. I finally agreed, but on the condition that I would send him a collection of souvenirs from the governor's office (non-taxpayer-funded, of course!). After thirty years, the little guitar from J. C. Penney was back home. When the Old State House Museum in Little Rock wanted personal items of governors for display, I loaned them the guitar, and if you are ever in Little Rock, you can stop by and see it. And as for the Gretsch Tennessean and Jazz Bass that I sold, after my kids were grown,

I scoured Internet sites and looked in every music store and pawnshop I could find whenever I was in a new town to try to find guitars like those. Though I spent a lot more than I got for the originals, I now own a 1964 Gretsch Tennessean (even more valuable than the one I had) and had Fender build a Jazz Bass exactly like the one I had when I was a teenager. They sit side by side next to my desk now, and seeing them makes me feel seventeen all over again. Then I stand up and realize I'm *not* seventeen again!

3.

Loneliness

I never knew my grandfather on my mother's side of the family. From what sparse descriptions I had of him from my mother, it sounded like it was just as well. She didn't talk about him much, and when she did, it was not with affection, but rather with a level of contempt that probably hid a lot of stuff I didn't need to know. She did tell me that he was an alcoholic and that he could often be harsh, even abusive. But in general, my mother buried her memories of her father deep within her soul and never, to my knowledge, talked about them to anyone. Her generation didn't have Oprah or Dr. Phil leading people to bare their souls and openly express all their inner feelings and emotions to the world. From what I gather, my grandfather's story would have been more fitting for *Jerry Springer* than *Oprah* anyway.

My grandfather was born in 1868 and died in 1945—ten

years before I was born. He served in the military during the Spanish-American War but was too old to fight in World War I. He had been married once before he married my grandmother and was almost sixty when my mother was born. He was considerably older than my grandmother but managed to father seven children with her. My mother was the oldest and therefore had the most memories of him—memories, it seems, she would later try to forget. In my grandfather's first marriage, he had fathered two sons, both of whom were easily old enough to be my mother's father. One of these two half brothers of hers, Garvin Elder, was the closest thing to an actual father figure she had.

To my sister and me, he was "Uncle Garvin." He was a lifelong bachelor who lived by himself in Houston, Texas. He had spent most of his career as an accountant for Armour Meat Company, and I suppose because he lived very frugally and never married or had kids, he kept most of what he earned for himself. He bought stock in the Gillette Company and kept up every day with the stock market. Although he led a generally simple life, he wore a suit, a starched white shirt, and a tie wherever he went. That meant he really stood out when he came to Hope for a visit, because no one in my entire family wore white starched shirts, let alone ties or suits.

Uncle Garvin didn't own a car, so he walked or took a city bus pretty much wherever he wanted to go in Houston. When he came to visit us, he almost always came on the Continental Trailways bus, which stopped only a couple of blocks from our house. When he arrived, either he'd walk from the bus stop or one of my parents would be waiting at the station to pick him up and drive him back to our house.

Uncle Garvin came to visit every Christmas, at least once during the summer, and often at Thanksgiving. Since he was more like our grandfather than an uncle, his visits were always special and always predictable. Within an hour of his arrival, he would walk to the neighborhood Kroger grocery store less than a block from our house and buy a whole chicken. That wasn't because he needed to buy his own food; there would be no "Starvin' Garvin" at our house! On the contrary, this was his not-so-subtle way of telling my mother what he wanted for dinner his first night with us—her fried chicken.

Don't think for a minute we minded a bit. To this day, I have never had fried chicken any better than what my mother made. If Colonel Sanders had had her recipe, he would have been a four-star general! Fried chicken, mashed potatoes and gravy, navy beans (this was a must-have!), and homemade biscuits with sweet tea were as predictable for Uncle Garvin's first meal at our house as Christmas coming on December 25 each year.

Even when he was just hanging out at our house during the day, Uncle Garvin still wore a starched white shirt and a tie. I thought that meant he must be important and intelligent, since he was the only person we knew who dressed up for work every day. Most of the men in my extended family didn't even own a suit, and those who did wore it only to funerals. When you saw any of my male relatives in a suit, you didn't ask what important event they were going to attend, you simply asked who had died and hoped it wasn't someone that you knew very well. Death in the family always meant two things—men who looked ridiculously uncomfortable and out of place in a suit would try to wear one, and people from the church and neighborhood would bring over a big bowl of potato salad. This was so predictable that when someone died, we rarely used words like dead, death, and passed away. We just said it was "potato salad time."

We usually knew what time the bus that brought Uncle Garvin "home" for Christmas was supposed to arrive, so sometime before that, my sister and I would park ourselves in the front yard and wait and watch for Uncle Garvin to appear. It was a big deal when one of us saw him first and started screaming, "Uncle Garvin! Uncle Garvin!" He and the well-traveled but stately brown suitcase in his hand were a welcome sight for us. These were the days long before luggage had wheels, and his suitcase was made of tan leather, which alone was reason enough to think he was pretty important. The only suitcase we had in our family was an old, beat-up one made of a stiff cardboardlike material. We never used it because we never really went anywhere to stay overnight. Uncle Garvin even had a luggage tag with his name on it, which was a sure sign that he was somebody special.

Uncle Garvin's visits meant that there would be an adult in the house all day, even when the parents were both at work. Other than his absolute and unbreakable appointment to watch Perry Mason on the old black-and-white TV, there was lots of time for us to challenge him to countless games of checkers. I truly believe that much of my own competitive spirit was developed during those checkers sessions with Uncle Garvin, because the old man didn't really understand how impolite it was to beat the daylights out of a sensitive little boy like me in a board game. Uncle Garvin played to win, and he usually did, until, after getting beat by him over and over, I got better and eventually even learned to beat him occasionally. At the time, I hated that he made easy play of me and actually seemed to relish beating a little kid in checkers, but in reality, he did me a great favor by making me hungry for victory and giving me the greatest thrill of all when I finally achieved it. This might be hard to believe for many of the hand-wringing whiners out there today who are so afraid of injuring a child's self-esteem that they've created a society in which "everyone gets a trophy" and no one loses no matter how little they practiced or how poorly they performed. This is the recipe for creating incompetent CEOs who, when their companies fail miserably, rush to the government to rescue them because they are "too big to fail." It's also created total idiots in government who think they are doing these poor businesses, as well as the rest of us, a favor by bailing out the losers at the expense of the winners so everything will be "fair." Call me crazy, but I believe there's something to be said for competition and for rewarding hard work, talent, and intelligence instead of laziness, incompetence, and stupidity.

Not that Uncle Garvin was mindfully trying to build in me an obsession with excellence or a hunger to succeed, but he stoked a fire in me to learn from failure and to ultimately believe that my greatest victories were the ones that followed a string of failures against the same foe. I'm lucky. I had someone who taught me this valuable lesson as a kid. Some parents today try to shield their children from the "pain and trauma" of losing. I don't think they realize that no matter how hard they try, these kids are going to grow up one day and learn this lesson the hard way. But by that time they'll be unprepared to face failure. God help us!

Since Uncle Garvin didn't own a car, he walked a lot. It's not like he couldn't afford a car, but I think in his mind, it was an expense he could do without. When he was at our house, it meant that we walked a lot too, because if we were going to hang out with him, we would spend a good part of the day walking around town to do whatever errands there were to do.

A part of Uncle Garvin's daily routine was walking to Jack's News Stand on the corner of First Street and Main just across the street from the Missouri Pacific train depot in Hope. Jack's was a grimy little store that always smelled like cigars and fresh popcorn. Cigars and popcorn don't make the most desirable aroma, but they sure create a memorable one! Jack's was Hope's main place to buy newspapers other than the local daily paper, *The Hope Star*, which was so small that instead of being rolled, it was often folded wallet size so it could be thrown easily by the kids on bikes who delivered the paper each afternoon. To get "real" papers, like the ones from Little Rock, Shreveport, or Texarkana, one had to go to Jack's. This was also true for magazines like *Time*, *Newsweek*, or *U.S. News & World Report*, although in those days, more people read *Life*, *Look*, and *Reader's Digest* (two of which don't even exist now). Jack's also had racy magazines like *Playboy*, which were kept behind the counter. Young guys knew they were there, but they also knew that if they attempted to buy one in the name of their "dad" or "older brother," Jack, the proprietor, would simply ask "Dad's" name (though he probably already knew it, since Hope was so small) and pick up the phone to call to see if he really wanted his son to pick up a *Playboy*. The only future in that exchange would be an old-fashioned "whipping" with a belt or, even worse, one of the hideous green tree branches affectionately known as switches. I'm sure I'm offending the sensibilities of those who think corporal punishment a form of barbarism, but it never occurred to me at the time to think of myself as being abused. I was simply experiencing my early indoctrination into my father's form of patriotism—true patriotism—he laid on the stripes and I saw stars.

After we walked to Jack's so my uncle could pick up a copy of the *New York Times*, *Houston Post*, or *Shreveport Times* to check the stock market and get the news, we'd walk back home and sometimes stop at Joe's City Bakery for a chocolate-covered doughnut. On the way back, since the fire station where my dad worked was only two blocks from our house, we'd usually stop there to see him if he was working that day. On afternoon walks, we sometimes walked the eight or ten blocks to the local Dairy Queen, which meant a soft-serve ice cream cone.

It was fun walking with Uncle Garvin because he didn't poke around. His walks were brisk, and walking around Hope with a man all dressed up in a suit and, usually, a light tan fedora made us feel like real big shots. He even wore what we called old man socks, which were actually midcalf silk stockings, but since all we knew were white cotton socks (even with jackets and ties), even those seemed pretty upscale.

The visits with Uncle Garvin were some of our favorite times of the year, but they weren't without some moments of frustration. He was more predictable than the Cubs losing to the Cardinals, and because he was an eccentric and lifelong bachelor, he was used to having things his way and on his own terms. He wanted his meals prepared so specifically that one would have thought he was ordering from the menu at the Four Seasons, and we always watched what he wanted to watch on TV, which meant that during his visits, Popeye cartoons and *The Three Stooges* had to give way to *The Edge of Night*, the evening news, and the aforementioned *Perry Mason*. Years later, as an adult, my wife and I would come to love watching *Perry Mason* reruns late at night, but I confess that it took me a while to get over my loathing of the show that I had been force-fed by Uncle Garvin when I would have rather been watching *The Little Rascals*.

It seemed that the regular visits from Uncle Garvin would always be a part of our lives, especially at Christmas. We always looked forward to Uncle Garvin's Christmas visits most because they were the longest and my sister and I were out of school and had more time to be home. Plus, Uncle Garvin would always give us a five-dollar bill as a gift, which for us was a lot of cold cash to have, since back then a movie ticket only cost twenty-five cents and a hamburger at Dad's Hamburger Stand only cost a dime.

Uncle Garvin was as much a part of Christmas for us as the tree and the ornaments. That is, until the Christmas of 1967.

In the fall of 1967, I noticed that my mother and dad had several phone calls with Uncle Garvin. That was unusual because in those days most of the communication between Uncle Garvin and my mother was through typed letters, his typed on old-fashioned tissue-thin typing paper on an old Underwood Five machine, and my mother's also banged out on an Underwood with a hand-operated carriage return and a little bell that rang at the end of a line of type. Long-distance phone calls were rare at my house and were done by dialing zero on the phone and telling the operator, "I'd like to make a *long-distance call*," which sounded about as important as launching a satellite into orbit. Receiving a long-distance call was just as big a deal, and whoever answered the phone would run about the house shouting, "Long distance! Long distance!" All of this seems so long ago in the age of cell phones, instant messaging, and text messaging, but back then, the fact that a simple voice call from another city was occurring seemed like a really big deal that stopped everything in its tracks.

A few of those calls, more letters than usual, and worried looks on my mother's face finally culminated in my parents' sitting down with my sister and me and giving us news that would forever change our lives and our Christmases.

Uncle Garvin had cancer.

Cancer is a horrible word now, but in 1967, it was pretty much the same as death. When we heard of people getting cancer, we never asked, "Did they catch it early enough?" but rather, "How long does he have?"

My mother told us that all those calls and letters were not only about the fact that Uncle Garvin had been diagnosed with cancer but also about what to do about it. The good news was that he lived in Houston, home to some of the world's best healthcare specialists as well as the M. D. Anderson Cancer Center. The bad news was that his doctors had told him that his lymphoma was incurable and none of their treatments would help him.

My mother told us that Uncle Garvin would be coming to live with us full time because he had no place to go and would need increasing care during whatever time he had left.

Our house wasn't very large to begin with, so having him come to live meant we had to make some major adjustments to accommodate more than the usual Christmas visit. My parents moved from their room into my sister's room, and she and I shared space in the attic, which had been somewhat walled off to create a makeshift room. There was a partition that gave us somewhat separate spaces, but we had very little privacy.

Having a dying man come to live with us meant much more to my sister and me than just a move to the attic. We could no longer have friends over because it might disturb Uncle Garvin, and we had to cease playing music at high volume. By this time, I was very much into my guitar, playing with a band, and loving not having parents home in the afternoons so I could play loudly, so this was a very hard transition for me. It also meant that we'd have to help out more around the house, and we'd also have to assist in caregiving once we got home from school and before our parents could be home.

Instead of taking the bus to our house like he usually did, Uncle Garvin flew from Houston to Texarkana that November, and my dad drove the thirty miles to the airport to pick him up and bring him to what would be his home for the last few months of his life. When the car pulled into our driveway, we rushed out to meet him, and from that very first moment, I knew things weren't the same. While he was clearly trying to act chipper, there was a pained expression in his face that I had never seen, and he seemed frail. The confidence he had always exuded in his upright posture and meticulous grooming weren't as evident, and that would be the best he looked until the day he died.

My mother, of course, prepared the normal welcome-home dinner of fried chicken, mashed potatoes, and all the accompaniments, and this time Uncle Garvin didn't even have to stop at the store to ensure the menu. My sister and I had been told over and over again not to overload him with questions, especially about his cancer, but to try to just act like everything was normal.

From the very first meal, however, there was nothing normal about it. He had come with two suitcases this time instead of one, and many of his other things were on their way in a Bekins moving truck that would arrive a few days later. After he put his things in his room, we all gathered at the kitchen table for our first meal together as a now-extended family.

We had barely gotten under way with loading our plates and starting to eat when I heard Uncle Garvin call my mother's name. I saw a strange look on his face and sat stunned as he tried unsuccessfully to hold back vomit. After a scramble to get a pan, a bucket, a trash can—anything—I saw something I'd never seen before in this man of strength and steely resolve. He cried.

And inside, so did I.

Other relatives had died, but most of them were more distant—great-uncles or great-aunts who were old and passed away, and a few younger ones who died suddenly of a heart attack or even in a car wreck. Yet in all those instances, we didn't really see the process of death—just the aftermath. Even on the death of my dad's aunt Clara, who committed suicide, we learned what happened from our parents, but in a sanitized version, and while we went to the funeral home for the obligatory visitation and then to the funeral, the whole process was rather calm even though surreal and unsettling. This was different. Death didn't get announced to us at breakfast one morning or after a phone call, and we weren't shielded from any of the grim details. We would watch as death slowly took each bit of strength and dignity from a man who had always represented to us nothing but strength and dignity.

I will never forget the look of humiliation on my uncle's face after that moment at the dinner table. If he had ever had a moment of weakness or fear or vulnerability, we'd never seen it, and he was clearly embarrassed that he had ruined a meal for us and had been unable to maintain his rigid and erudite Methodist deportment.

He lost more than his dinner that night. He lost what he valued more than his Gillette stock—he lost his independence. And I lost more than the privacy of a room; I lost my childhood innocence.

I had always envied my Uncle Garvin because of his stubborn independence. Since he had no wife or kids, he answered to no one except himself. If he wanted to go somewhere, do something, or buy something, he only had to take his own counsel. I always thought he had it great, but that night I realized that he also had something I'd never known before—he had loneliness.

It had never occurred to me before that being independent and unencumbered by other people's schedules, likes and dislikes, and needs also meant not having the stability of knowing that there would be someone around to share your burdens or help shoulder your load.

My parents hired a young woman named Margaret Wilson to come and help take care of my uncle during the day when they were working and we were at school. She would come in the mornings and leave not too long after my sister and I came home. After she left, it was my sister's and my responsibility to take care of things until one of our parents got home. We loved Margaret. She was afraid of nothing, full of spunk and inexhaustible joy, and as a bonus, she was a wonderful cook. That was helpful to my uncle but also took a big burden off my mother. If Margaret had to leave early, my sister and I would prepare meals, clean, and provide care.

In the four months that Uncle Garvin lived with us until he died, I had to do a lot of growing up. My entire family was pretty much consumed with taking care of an eccentric and at times demanding man whom we watched slowly deteriorate from a virile and proud man who needed nothing to a fragile, weak, and broken man who could no longer bathe, shave, or dress himself on his own. This left an indelible impression on me as a twelve-year-old kid, and some of the sights, sounds, and smells of those days are scratched deep in my soul. Some things hadn't changed. We still had a tree, but the fresh pine smell was covered by the ever-present odor of Pine-Sol, which we constantly used to clean and cover up the hideous smell of sickness and impending death, a smell that is still etched into my memory.

We all knew that the Christmas of 1967 would be our last Christmas with Uncle Garvin, and so did he. I think in many ways we all tried to savor every moment of it by doing normal things like playing Christmas music on the record player and baking Christmas cookies, but at the same time there was an unspoken but vivid resentment that a person who was a major part of our lives was being taken from us by an insidious disease that cruelly devoured his life by the spoonful instead of allowing him to die quietly and with dignity. As the disease got stronger, Uncle Garvin's strength to fight it dwindled, until he ultimately surrendered any vestige of volition and became little more than a swollen human form animated by his breathing and heartbeat but barely resembling the person we knew him to be.

For him to summon us to his room for assistance, we devised a simple signal. We took a stainless-steel bowl from my mother's kitchen that when struck with a wooden spoon loudly pierced through whatever chatter might be going on in the house. It was our substitute for a bell. Some days it seemed that Uncle Garvin banged that bowl just to see how quickly we would come and to make sure we were still there in case he really needed us. I came to hate the sound of it because it meant not only that I had to abruptly stop whatever I was doing but also that I might have to face some unpleasant and unthinkable task like emptying a bedpan or cleaning up vomit or feces. Sometimes he would summon me just to turn the channel on the little black-and-white television set that he had had shipped with his belongings from Houston. (These were the days before remote controls.) As much as I feel guilty for all the anger and selfishness I felt at the time, to this day, there are some bells I hear at Christmas that sound like that bowl being struck, and instead of feeling "joy to the world," I cringe with haunting memories of Uncle Garvin's last Christmas.

It would be years before I came to realize that he didn't strike that bowl and have us running to his side simply because he wanted us to refresh his water, fiddle around with the covers on his bed, or rearrange the newspapers in the room. That bowl was a cry for something far more important; it was a call for the presence of another human being in that room so that he wouldn't spend those awful and painful waking moments with a condition worse than a cancer—loneliness.

Here was a man who lived alone his entire adult life and did what he wanted to do when he wanted to do it and the way he wanted to do it. He was with people when he wanted to be, like at the holidays, but when he left he had no responsibility for what happened after that. That level of autonomy was wonderful so long as he had his strength and control over his life. His transition from total independence to total dependence was sudden, stark, and most likely terrifying to him.

All the previous Christmases he had spent with us had been on his terms. He came when he decided to. He left when he decided to. He ordered the schedule and even the menu as he decided to. His last Christmas with us was unlike any other. But as I reflect upon it, despite the many challenges that we faced as a family, it was the best Christmas we had with him. We got up early as usual, and he made his way into the family room, where the tree was. Ordinarily, he would have already been showered, shaved, and dressed in his stately blue suit and tie, but on this day, he came in a robe and would shave later when my mother or dad could do it for him. We should all have received Oscars for acting as if everything were normal, but in fact, there was nothing normal about it.

In Uncle Garvin's final days, we were able to show him that he was more than the rich (at least by our standards) and particular uncle who came to visit a few times a year. He was very much a part of the family, a man for whom we set aside our lives to make sure his last days were not spent alone. We did the most menial and at times unpleasant and degrading tasks to make sure he was comfortable.

In so many ways, I became a man that year. I was forced to face the realities of death and the uncertainties of life. I saw life in its ugliest form, when a disease robs a person of his strength, his pride, his privacy, and his ability to choose even the simplest things. More than being robbed of my youth, I was endowed with an extra dose of maturity and adulthood the very year I would become a teenager, 1968.

Uncle Garvin lived through Christmas and died on April 6, 1968, when in the early morning hours of that day, two days exactly after the assassination of Dr. Martin Luther King Jr., the voice of my dad woke me up as he climbed to the top of the attic stairs to tell me that Uncle Garvin had just died. He wouldn't be alone ever again. But there was some satisfaction as the years went by that in those last four months of his life, he knew the love of a family that gave him a Christmas gift that was unlike any other we had ever given him. As best we knew how, we gave him the comfort of simple companionship even if it was sometimes difficult. Those last four months, he held to his faith and never once blamed God for his pain or acted or spoke with bitterness. But I'm certain that if we hadn't taken him into our home, he would have died even sooner and experienced more pain than he did.

God gives us many things, but the message of Christmas is that He loves us in person. His comfort wasn't just in the pages of a book or the "vibes" of a spiritual experience. It was with hands that touched, arms that hugged, a voice that spoke, and eyes that exuded compassion that He showed us how much He loved us.

My sister and I didn't get much that year for Christmas. We had been prepared to not expect much because all our resources needed to be used to care for Uncle Garvin and there really wasn't time for much else. But in many ways, it was one of our most meaningful Christmas experiences ever, not because it was a happy one, but because it wasn't. It was meaningful because through it we learned that the real meaning of Christmas is not giving toys but giving God's grace in person to someone who is no longer in a position to give back. It was a very simple Christmas, and maybe the best one of all.

4.

Family

"Son, don't look too far up that family tree—
there's stuff up there you don't need to see."

With that, my dad pretty well summed up much of the family history. Don't get me wrong. There were certainly some admirable branches and twigs in that tree, but the family on both sides had plenty of scoundrels. It's a miracle I ever got elected to anything. I think the local papers were too busy trying to conjure up controversy over idiotic nonsense like what we were eating at the Governor's Mansion to bother doing real investigations into my bloodline.

In my family, like most others, Christmas was the one time of year when we saw relatives we usually only saw at family reunions. Neither side of my family was particularly religious, so it was somewhat ironic that we made such a big deal out of a holiday that celebrates the birth of Jesus, seeing as no one ever really talked about Him at any other time of the year. It wasn't that the clans were atheist or hostile to faith, they just weren't really gung ho about the idea of getting dressed up on Sundays for church. That made sense, seeing as no one really had dress clothes, and in those days, people wore their "Sunday best" to church. Among the adult men in our family, "Sunday best" wasn't really any different from "Monday best." Kids usually had at least one white shirt and a clip-on black tie just for special events at school or a Christmas program at church.

Many of the stories in this book only make sense if you know a little bit about my family. Brace yourself! I'm about to take you on a journey that has a not-so-noble beginning but is still truly remarkable and proves the power of perseverance and the presence of hope.

As best I can tell, the Huckabee side of the family originated in England, around the Liverpool area, and the name means "people of the hill." I actually looked it up once while visiting Liverpool, and that's the best I can figure. I was hoping I might be related to Paul McCartney, John Lennon, George Harrison, or Ringo Starr, but if there's any connection, they have long since paid to cover it up. When I was a kid, I had heard that the Huckabees were of Irish descent, but during a 2009 trip to Ireland, my research revealed that the Irish claimed no responsibility. They did acknowledge that some of those English Huckabees might have slipped across the Irish Sea, but they were pretty sure they were turned away and sent swimming back home.

I do know that the Sons of the American Revolution have never called and said they would love to have me. My folks didn't come over on the Mayflower, and their first American address was not Jamestown but Georgia, as best we know. I assume that means they were dumped out of debtor prisons in the old country, placed on boats like cargo, and dropped off on the Georgia shores to fend for themselves. That's not altogether a bad thing, since the clan did turn out to be a resourceful and resilient lot despite the fact that they were poorer than the dirt they lived on for most later generations. If there was a rich Huckabee in my ancestry, it was a better-kept secret than the whereabouts of Jimmy Hoffa. I'm sure there wasn't one, but if there was he probably would have kept it quiet to avoid having the rest of the family move in and rob him blind.

I can't verify the veracity of some things I've been told, for example, that some of my ancestors were horse thieves or that more than one Huckabee concluded his life at the end of a rope, having been administered a rather outdated form of frontier justice. When asked about these stories, I prefer to say that "they were participating in a public ceremony when the platform on which they were standing suddenly gave way and they were killed almost instantly." (That level of creative "spin" came in very useful in my life as a political figure!)

Supposedly, once those early Huckabees landed in the young and still-developing United States in the late 1700s, they scattered like fugitives to places like Arkansas, Louisiana, and Alabama, with some staying in Georgia. Because they weren't well educated and couldn't spell much better than they could avoid the long arm of the law, there were (and are) many variations of the spelling of the name "Huckabee." I want to point that out so you don't think that the variations were simply aliases. I've seen it spelled Huckaby, Huckabay, Huckabe, and Huckaba. There are probably other spellings, but those folks probably don't want to claim kin to me any more than the rest of them.

Because my name is somewhat unusual, I was instructed not to immediately say yes when someone asked if I was "kin to the Huckabees who lived in Albany, Georgia" (or anywhere else, for that matter). I was told that I shouldn't volunteer that information until I knew why I was being asked. "There's a good chance that the other Huckabees owed those folks some money, and they might be expecting you to pay up," my dad said. So, if your name is Huckabee (or any variation of it), unless you have photos of us together at Christmas, I don't know you and we aren't related. (But we probably are!)

But speaking of Christmas, isn't it funny that at Christmas people we barely know pile in and get chummy for a big meal, or even a few days, when we'd all probably find it easier to hang out with coworkers or neighbors, since we really know them better than we do our relatives. It's awkward for all, and yet in a strange kind of way, it wouldn't be Christmas without the obligatory connection with family members—even the ones we barely know. These are the people to whom we are genetically linked. We can look at our older relatives and get a glimpse of how we might look someday (*yikes!*), and when we look at the younger ones, we might remember how we once looked. But beyond physical appearances and behavioral traits, there is that reassuring reminder that we are in fact a part of an ongoing chain of human life—there is continuity in our existence, and continuity means purpose, and if we have a purpose, then surely that's an affirmation that we were created by something larger than ourselves and aren't mere products of chance and accident. (Although I'm sure that some of my relatives must have looked at me and thought God did have a great sense of humor!)

Enough of my deep thoughts on the nature and role of families. Let's face it, at Christmas, even if we believe in creation, we might become convinced that we're all devolving.

My family has given me lots of material for several books, but since a bunch of them are still living, I can't tell all the stories I have. Instead, I will have to limit the Christmas memories to those that won't get me sued or, worse, beaten to a pulp by more violent members of my bloodline.

On my mother's side of the family, the Elders, Christmas was complicated because my mother was one of seven children. This meant that whatever we did, it was going to be crowded. One of her brothers, Neal Elder, died before I was even born, and it was tragic. He drowned the day before his wedding. He was second in age to my mother, and they were close, so his death was one she never really got over. It also meant that she was terrified of our drowning. But even with Uncle Neal gone, that still left six siblings, and after they all married and had kids, whoever's house we went to for Christmas was going to be filled beyond capacity. None of my mother's family had large homes, but I don't think we ever even thought about that then. I do remember that almost all of the adults smoked. This was in the 1950s and early '60s, when it would've been unthinkable to suggest that blowing toxic carcinogens into the faces of children might be dangerous and maybe they should smoke outdoors. It didn't help that I was allergic to smoke (though we didn't know that then); any complaint that I couldn't breathe was met with a dismissive "Boy, quit your whining and acting up like that." It's a darn good thing no one had smoke alarms back then—they never would have stopped ringing.

In addition to celebrating the Elder family Christmas party in a room more crowded than the mosh pit at a Whitesnake concert and more smoke filled than the inside of a California wildfire, I had to put up with adults doing embarrassingly strange things either to get or to avoid attention. Looking back, I don't think anyone was normal.

First there was my grandmother, Eva Whitney Elder Garner. She was born a Whitney, married and widowed by an Elder, and married and abandoned or divorced (we're not sure which) by a Garner. The thing that distinguished my maternal grandmother was the fact that she had lost one eye as a young woman, supposedly by looking at the sun. She never bothered to get a glass eye or anything cosmetic such as a simple patch— she just had one good eye and one that just wasn't there. Her appearance scared little kids at first sight, but we were all used to it. The only thing more pronounced about her than her eye was her voice. It was loud. My cousin Sandy had dubbed her Go-Go, which stuck, because he said all she did was "go, go, go." So that's we called our grandma. Not "Grandma," "Granny," "Big Mama," or anything remotely normal for a grandparent. She was "Go-Go."

Go-Go couldn't see, and her sister, our aunt Mary, couldn't hear. Aunt Mary wasn't totally deaf, but it might have been better if she had been. She *thought* she could hear, so the rest of us had to scream at the top of our lungs to get through to her, and even then she might hear sounds but not necessarily understand them. And because she couldn't hear, she assumed we couldn't either, so she screamed as loudly to us as we did to her. When Aunt Mary was around, the house was louder than any concert Aerosmith ever played.

My sister and I were the oldest of the grandkids, so that meant we were assigned the duty of helping watch our younger cousins as they destroyed the house and all our toys while the adults indulged in nicotine and Maxwell House coffee, which was always kept cooking in the old-fashioned stainless-steel percolator. It was a darned good thing that we were apt to get some new toys at Christmas because the ones we had took a beating from the not-so-gentle handling of our cousins.

Cheap Kodak black-and-white Brownie cameras with those onetime-use, hot-to-the-touch flashbulbs were going off constantly in an effort to record these wonderful moments together so we could one day look back on them with fondness. The food was phenomenal, and I later came to realize that back then in the deep, impoverished South, there may not have been new cars or nice homes, but by gosh, there was great food. Each family who piled in for the event had a special and traditional item they brought to the gathering. I could always count on Aunt Mary to bring her "famous" popcorn balls. I'm sure you've heard about those popcorn balls—she always claimed they were her "famous" version, after all. I'm not sure what made them famous or who outside our immediate family ever tried them, but no matter, they were famous in our house.

My mother's sister Elsie rivaled my mother as an excellent cook, and the Elder family events were generally held at our house, hers, or Go-Go's. As small as Elsie's and our houses were, they were palatial compared to the tiny two-bedroom cottage that my grandmother occupied. Think college frat boys crammed in a phone booth and you've got an accurate picture of Go-Go's house at Christmas. Elsie made great vegetables, which she took from her own garden and canned in the summer, and some killer fudge. My mother would make chicken, roast beef, and corn bread so good that to this day, I feel completely ripped off when I'm served corn bread anywhere else. My mother's was all from scratch, and she never used a recipe but was still somehow always consistent.

Because there were so many of us and none of us were affluent enough to afford gifts for everyone, the tradition was to draw names from a bowl to determine who you would buy a gift for. Kids drew kids' names and adults drew adults' names. I wasn't concerned with the name I drew, since our parents would get the gift anyway, but I watched with intensity to see who drew my name, because that would determine if I had something to look forward to for next Christmas or not—some of the cousins were known to bring really worthless trinkets that wouldn't last through the Christmas party. I even tried to find a way to rig the drawing, which I never figured out how to do. I think it's one of the reasons I became a Republican instead of a Democrat; I just wasn't able to get the whole ballot-box-stuffing, election-fraud game mastered.

There were advantages and disadvantages to hosting the Elder family party. The advantage of staying at home was that we didn't have to be cramped up in Go-Go's house, which was like trying to fit the entire Kennedy clan in a nineteen-foot RV, or drive to the country, where Elsie lived, where we would be forced to stay until my parents were finally worn out and ready to go home. Another advantage of having it at our house was that we'd have more leftover food, I knew the places I could hide to get away from people or the never-ending cigarette smoke, and I wouldn't fall asleep on the way home only to be rudely awakened and have to stagger into the house and fall asleep all over again.

The main disadvantage of making our house the "scene of the crime" was that my cousins would ruthlessly test every last one of my toys to the limits of their durability and leave a trail of clutter and mayhem that I would have to clean up. I tried to avoid this by hiding stuff I really cared about and leaving out only what I thought was indestructible. The other disadvantage was that we couldn't just pack up and leave when we wanted to and had to wait until everyone ate themselves into a sugar-coated and caffeine-induced stupor and had the good sense to leave.

Some in the family had to travel from places like Fort Worth, Texas, or Ohio (or wherever the air force had stationed my aunt Vena's husband, Roger), but the rest were from around Hope, so the only person we usually had to accommodate for the night was Uncle Garvin. Pat and I loved him, and he never played with or broke our toys, so it was a good deal all the way.

My aunt Louise was married to Jack Casey, and they lived in Texas, where he was from. He scared the living daylights out of me because he was a giant of a man—probably six foot six in a day when tall men were maybe five foot ten. He was tall and big and a stern disciplinarian. My parents were pretty strict too, but they weren't so tall that they had to literally duck to go through a door, like he did, so they weren't as intimidating. Because Uncle Jack and Aunt Louise's three kids were closest in age to my sister and me, we probably played with them most and were closest to them even though we saw them only at Christmas and sometimes Easter. As fierce and imposing as Uncle Jack was, Aunt Louise was soft-spoken, even tempered, and ever so calm. When Janet and I married and later lived in Fort Worth, we were able to see the Caseys more often, and I was amazed by how tame Uncle Jack was. Maybe as a child I thought he was the giant from "Jack and the Beanstalk" or the guy who David had to take down with a sling, but it turned out he was the "gentle giant" after all.

My aunt Elsie and her husband Alvin presented the most interesting of family connections. She was my mother's sister, but her husband was Alvin Huckabee, my dad's cousin. His dad and my grandfather were brothers. It gets worse—his mother and my grandmother were sisters. Unravel the string in all this and no one actually married a sister or even a cousin, but it was about as close as a bloodline could get without dipping into a very shallow gene pool. In the old days, when people in my grandparents' day were "courting," there was usually only one horse-driven wagon per family. When one of the males went to see a female, the siblings rode along and could choose someone from the same farm to date if they wanted—quite a limited selection! There were no cell phones then, and most of my relatives didn't own cars until the 1930s or later, so we ended up with some close calls on genetic separation. That meant that my cousin Sandy Carl and his sister Cindy are my first, double second, and third cousins. Make fun of me if you want to, but if I ever need someone to donate a kidney to me, just think of the possibilities of a genetic match!

There was also my aunt Emilie and her husband Leon, whom we liked because he was a cop and would put handcuffs on us so we could see what they felt like (not too pleasant, actually). Given the notorious stories of our ancestors, I suppose there was some part of us that figured we needed to get used to the feel just in case we repeated history!

The youngest of the Elder offspring was Uncle Junior. He was actually William Thomas Elder Jr., which sounded more distinguished, but I wasn't aware that he had a name other than "Junior" until I was in high school. He had served briefly in the Marine Corps and had played drums in the high-school band but never graduated.

Since my mother was the oldest, after she finished high school, she went straight to work to help provide for the family. This was especially important at that time because her father was dying and leaving them with more needs and fewer resources. Three of my aunts, Louise, Elsie, and Emilie, were able to do what my mother wanted but never got to do—go to college. Louise and Elsie were both schoolteachers, and Emilie worked in a law office.

Christmas on the Huckabee side of the family was much less complicated. My dad had only one sister, and she was fifteen years younger than him. My paternal grandparents lived directly across the street from us, so we saw them every day. My great-grandfather was Lucious Huckabee—a name I'd never heard before, nor have I ever heard it since, considering probably no one ever thought to name their kid after him. He was most charitably described as a "rascal." That was just a nicer way of saying that he was a woman-chasing, heavy-drinking, hard-living, and hot-tempered old man who had succeeded in alienating himself from all of his children during the course of his lifetime. That didn't seem to affect his health, however, as he lived to be more than a hundred years old. I tried to hide this story from my children out of fear that they might assume that the path to longevity is drinking, fighting, cussing, smoking, and abandoning one's family responsibilities. I met him on several occasions, but my memories of him are limited and not especially fond. My grandfather never spoke of him—ever. He and my grandfather had it out when my grandfather was a young man, and as soon as my grandfather was old enough, he ran away, joined the navy, and served on a destroyer during World War I. After he came home from the navy, he went to work at the Hope Brick Works, where he worked until his retirement. His was a simple life—he worked eighty hours a week (at least six days a week) and due to stomach ulcers ate only green pea soup and saltines. I mean, literally, that's what he ate every day, except at breakfast, when he ate Grape-Nuts cereal. He worked in a hot and sweaty environment, baking bricks and doing a lot of heavy lifting and hard "he-man" work. He always smelled like a combination of green pea soup and Absorbine Jr., a rub-on potion that was supposed to ease the soreness in his overused muscles. The only other medicine he believed in was a combination of WD-40 and Dr. Tichenor's. Dr. Tichenor's was an "old school" all-purpose elixir that was actually nothing but alcohol and strong peppermint oil, but my grandfather swore by both. He used the WD-40 on his elbows and knees as a "joint lubricant" and believed that it was much better than any other painkiller on the market.

Because so many of the Huckabees were estranged from my great-grandfather, and my grandfather and grandmother only had two kids, Christmas on that side of the family was much easier. A few gifts to open with a small gathering of the immediate family was about all there was to the Huckabee Christmas.

As the years went by, families grew and scattered, life became more complicated, and the older relatives died off, the annual Christmas gatherings of the Elder family ended. At the time, I was glad because it meant fewer broken toys and tobacco-puffing adults filling up a house telling the same old, tired stories about their childhood that everyone had heard a million times. But now I realize that had it not been for those evenings of storytelling and embellishing the tales of our ancestors, we would have had no real connection to who we were, where we had come from, and what made us the way we were. I'm sure that somewhere there are sociologists and anthropologists who might find deeper meaning in all of those stories and the people behind them. Those stories helped me understand a vital truth about who I was. As the prophet Isaiah said, "Look to the rock from which you were hewn; to the quarry from which you were dug." As my dad warned, there are things in that family tree I didn't need (or want) to see, and I have always hoped that others wouldn't see them either, but there are more things I'm happy to see, and in recent years, I've found myself looking for them more and more. Life then was not complicated by Xboxes, laptops, iPhones, or security checks at airports. In fact, there was no airport issue for me then, because I never imagined that I'd ever get to fly on a plane, much less live on one, which is more or less what I do now.

Back then we traveled by car, except for my Uncle Garvin, who came by bus. As the little house got increasingly crowded and the noise level increased, there was no irritation or sense of disruption, but rather a sense that this was what Christmas was all about. We weren't distracted by video games, the Internet, or high-def TV. Besides, the stories from our family were a lot more entertaining than anything on TV, especially back then, and instead of three channels, we had dozens of relatives to choose from who were more than happy to regale us with tales of yesteryear.

Life was pretty simple. It was just about family, mostly. And the family Christmas. Then, life was simple. The family wasn't, but Christmas was. Christmas might have seemed like a hassle back then—with the loud relatives, destructive cousins, and constant cigarette smoke, but looking back on it, I appreciate how genuine it was. Sure, my family may have been a bit complicated, but the Christmas was always simple.

5.

Traditions

Why do we do what we do at Christmas? Why do we do the same things the same way at the same time and with the same people? From the food we eat to the decorations we hang on the tree to the way we exchange gifts to the ritual of having one of the children in the family read the Christmas story from Luke 2, traditions are as much a part of what makes Christmas special as the meaning behind it. Those traditions give us comfort and familiarity and a sense of well-being. Traditions don't have to be fancy or costly— they just have to be consistent. We keep them because we need them to reassure us that, no matter how crazy our lives become and how many things change, there are some things that will stay the same, and those are the things that anchor us to who we are. The older I get, the more I cherish traditions, especially at Christmas.

I will spend more nights in a hotel this year than I will at home. Far more. Somewhere between 200 and 250 nights this year I will sleep in a hotel room and live like a vagabond—living out of a suitcase, dining on takeout, and hopping from airplane to airplane. I will, for the most part, stay in one of the Marriott brands for a reason that probably only makes sense to fellow frequent travelers. I choose Marriott because it's predictable, or, put another way, familiar.

When a person spends so much of his time changing cities, hotels, and locations on an almost nightly basis, it's a comfort to not have to totally reorient to the little things every day. I think I would be a great consultant to airlines and hotel chains because I could explain to them how to do a better job of keeping repeat customers! I don't care about beautiful lobbies and elaborate water features in the atrium—I want to be able to pull my bags into the room at the end of an exhausting day and have such a sense of familiarity that I don't feel disconnected from my routine.

I know that the room layout in a Courtyard by Marriott hotel is pretty much the same in Los Angeles as it is in Des Moines and Charlotte. I know how the clocks and TVs work; I know how many pillows I will have, what the shampoo and soap will be packaged in, and how the thermostat works. I know what kind of shower the room will have and what the towels will feel like. Same for the other Marriott brands, where there is an overall consistency from town to town, hotel to hotel, and room to room.

When I can't be home to enjoy the comfort and familiarity of my home and my family (my wife and three dogs), the least I can ask for is not having to waste any time relearning the nuances of a hotel in which I will only be staying a few hours. It's not nice artwork on the walls or elaborate fixtures that matter to me, but good Internet connections, quiet rooms, and people authorized to fix a problem on-site if it arises.

Essentially, it's creating a "tradition." We get comfort and a sense of calm from things happening the same way each time. It is the sociological equivalent of navigation points on our psychological GPS systems that tell us that, as long as at least some things stay constant in our lives, we are okay and things are on track.

This is especially important at Christmas, when we take the time to reconnect with people and reflect on our lives. Though we may have changed jobs, moved, had a health crisis, or experienced the death of a family member in the past year, Christmas traditions give us security and peace of mind. One of my close Catholic friends once explained to me why he loved and appreciated the very predictable and routine Catholic liturgy. He told me that no matter where in the world he was, he could go to a Catholic church and have the exact same service that he would have had at home. It was comforting to him that, in the midst of total turmoil and turbulence in the world, there was one place where the traditions gave him a deep sense of wholeness and tranquility. That made sense and helped me appreciate the attraction for many Catholics who take comfort in the fact that their church will be stable and constant. Since I come from the free-church model of evangelical theology, the constant in my church experience was the doctrine and the adherence to more rigid interpretations of the Bible. The church we attend is *very* nontraditional. The worship and music are contemporary—the polar opposite of the form of worship we had when we were younger. But even this modern church has traditions, or ways of doing things that are predictable and therefore comforting.

I've taken several trips across the state of Arkansas, from the northwest corner to the southeast corner, traveling solely by way of my BassCat bass boat. Navigating the Arkansas River for 308 miles is a wonderful experience and allows me to experience the sheer splendor of my state's beauty like no other method. But I know that I have to pay very careful attention to the red and green navigation markers in the navigable channel or risk running aground in shallows or hitting rock jetties under the surface. When we have no navigation markers to guide us, we can run aground.

Christmas traditions are a part of what keeps us "in the channel." I feel sorry for people who have no real Christmas traditions and wonder if they sometimes feel as though the holiday is just another hectic, confusing, and stressful time of year, rather than a peaceful and serene season.

Growing up, our family had traditions that provided a source of certainty in an otherwise uncertain world. From my earliest memories, I can remember the Saturday expedition that my dad and I would take a couple of weeks before Christmas for the annual Christmas tree hunt. We would go to my uncle's farm and traipse through the woods looking for a small cedar tree that we'd cut down, drag back to my dad's pickup truck, and haul home to be mounted in a bucket (that was its base) and decorated. The excursion meant I had to put on my little rubber boots to keep my feet warm and dry as we walked for a long time through pastures, fields, and forests until we found our Christmas tree. As I look at the photos from those days, it appears that our trees would make the Charlie Brown Christmas tree seem fit for the White House! But we were always proud to have it, and because we got it at my uncle's farm, it was free. I was always amazed that people went to Christmas tree lots and bought trees. I wanted to put my head out the truck window and scream, "People, there are trees in the woods!"

Most of the trees we had were cedar. I knew that the cedar branches could really irritate my arms when I had to handle the tree, but I was in my twenties when I found out that I was actually allergic to cedar trees! That's why my skin itched and my throat was scratchy and my nose was runny—Christmas was killing me.

While the "men" were out doing the "manly" task of chopping down one of God's trees, the "womenfolk" (mother and sister) stayed at home doing what they always did on that day—make divinity candy, chocolate chip cookies, and roasted pecans. The pecans were from our own two highly productive pecan trees, and the recipe to roast them is one I still use every year. It's one of the few recipes from my mother's mental library that I actually learned, and it turns out I'm not the only one who thinks those are the best roasted pecans ever. Every year when I make them, I'm told they are the best. (Of course, usually the people who tell me that are those who work for me and therefore aren't about to tell me that my pecans are garbage, but they *are* good.) Too bad I didn't learn the cookie or divinity recipe.

Once we had the scrawny little tree, which seemed big to me at the time, all set up, it was time to decorate. We had the same glass ornaments that had been carefully tucked away in boxes and stored in the attic from the year before. Seeing them each year gave me such a sense of comfort. Those delicate and colorful little balls of glass had survived another year, and so had we. The "girls" put the ornaments on, but first my dad wired up the lights. This meant rolling the string of lights out on the floor and testing the bulbs and replacing the ones that hadn't survived their year in storage. The most vivid Christmas memory my sister and I have is probably one of my dad, who one year accidently stuck his finger into an empty light socket and felt the full impact of 110 volts of electricity. He was momentarily frozen in a cartoonlike pose, eyes bugged out, uttering a profanity (I will spare you) that, due to the electricity, just dragged out for several seconds. Had it killed him, we probably wouldn't have found it so funny, but it didn't kill him. It nearly killed us, though, as we almost died with laughter listening to his electrically charged and elongated expression of a word that was a synonym for feces. I will use the more appropriate substitute but try to illustrate the sound in writing: "Shooooooooooooooooooooooooot!" Okay, you had to be there, but believe me when I tell you it was worth the price of that month's electric bill.

In addition to the trip to the woods for the tree and the decorations, Christmas was filled with other familiar traditions that I fondly recall and a few that I just recall, without so much fondness.

The Hope Fire Department hosted a Christmas dinner for

the firemen and their families each year. The fire trucks were moved outside of the station, and the entire interior was turned into a large dining hall with long tables set up for the big dinner, which included all the typical turkey and dressing, vegetables, and desserts imaginable. The big moment of the night was near the end, when Santa Claus himself came and gave every kid a great big peppermint candy cane. We also got to tell him what we wanted for Christmas, even though by that time I had already sent a letter to the North Pole and was somewhat disappointed that he didn't remember all that stuff I had listed. But this also gave me hope that he had forgotten what a little monster I had been throughout the year and that maybe he would cut me some slack and give me something better than the lump of coal I'd been threatened with. After Santa came with the candy, he headed back to the North Pole (it's a long trip from Arkansas, and he had a lot of toys left to make anyway). Then came the part that, as kids, we looked forward to even more than Santa—we got to take a ride around town on one of the big fire trucks and even got to ring the bell and blow the siren. I can only imagine the blistering press treatment a fire department would receive today if it loaded a bunch of kids onto a city-owned truck and drove them around town shattering the peace and quiet of the night with sirens and clanging bells. Not to mention the liability the department would incur for having those kids in the truck in the first place. Of course, those didn't even include the risks we took by repeatedly sliding down the big brass fire poles that connected the upstairs sleeping quarters to the area where the trucks were. One other thing happened at that firemen's supper that made it even more exciting—the firemen opened up the soft-drink machine and instead of making us pay ten cents for a Coke as usual, they would give them to us for *free*! How good could it get?

Back then Christmas traditions weren't limited to places of employment. In those days, schoolteachers didn't know what the ACLU was and would have laughed them out of town if they had dared suggest we stop singing Christmas carols, telling the Christmas story, or having a Christmas party in school. Every Christmas at Brookwood Elementary, which I attended through the sixth grade, each student in our class put their name in a bowl and then we all drew names to see who we would get a gift for. One of the kids in our class was a Jehovah's Witness, and since they don't observe Christmas celebrations, he was always excused from this drawing and didn't come to school on the day of the party. In today's world, his parents would have sued the bricks off the school, and we never would have had the Christmas party. None of us thought of it as a big deal that our classmate didn't participate and frankly respected the fact that he took his faith so seriously.

The teacher put limits on how much we could spend for each gift—never more than a dollar in the years I attended—so that everyone got an equally good gift. Of course, we always got the teacher something as well, but I don't recall what I ever got any of my teachers since my mother handled that—I just wanted to make sure that the gift I gave a classmate didn't make him cry because he thought it was crappy. And, of course, I hoped that the gift I received didn't make me cry because I thought it was crappy.

The only thing more exciting than being able to goof around

all day in school on the last day before Christmas break was knowing that we'd have two weeks out of school. It meant that Uncle Garvin would be coming for a visit and that we'd have more time to sneak open our presents during the day and play with them while our parents were still at work. Christmas vacation, here we come!

Of course, home, work, and school weren't the only places we had Christmas traditions. If there ever was a place where things stayed the same, it was church. They really couldn't afford to change anything about Christmas, which was fine by me. There was always a Christmas pageant where all the kids in Sunday school would sing a carol or two at a special service. It was one way of making sure all the parents showed up for church at least once a year, because they'd come to watch their kids sing even though they might not come and hear the preacher scream.

Preachers at my little Baptist church in those days tended to do a lot of screaming, which literally scared the hell out of me and also did a good job of keeping me wide awake. It didn't work for everyone, though. Because I couldn't understand all the sermon material, I would usually occupy my time by observing two men in our church. One was an older gentleman who loved church because apparently it was the best sleep he got all week. I think the preacher had to scream just to be heard over the sound of his snoring. (I would use names here, but there are families of these guys who are still around, and even though I don't think I could get sued for slander, why take the risk?) The other man said "Amen!" really loudly to basically everything the preacher said. I figured that was the stuff that was really good, since it evoked such a strong, outward, verbal affirmation from the man my sister and I affectionately called Mr. Amen. We would count the number of amens in a service, and it was about as accurate a way to judge the quality of the sermon as Siskel and Ebert's thumbs were to gauge the quality of a movie. I remember one nineteen-amen sermon, which set the record for amens in one service. Average amens were about twelve per Sunday.

Christmas church was different from regular Sunday church. The preacher didn't scream as much but instead read from either Luke 2 or the first couple of chapters of Matthew to tell the story that we already knew pretty well anyway. I kind of felt sorry for the preacher at Christmas because you could tell he was trying to make the story interesting so we'd respond more like Mr. Amen than like Mr. Rip Van Winkle. I also think he didn't scream because the whole sermon was about the "baby Jesus" and screaming at a baby just seemed a bit over the top.

For the church Christmas pageant, the kids gathered up bathrobes and broom handles from home and used them to dress up like the shepherds and the wise men. Later I found out that the real wise men in the story were rich big shots, while the shepherds were poor and smelled like their sheep. But in our pageants, they all looked and smelled pretty much the same. Whichever older girl in our church could sit still the longest got to be Mary. She had to pretty much sit in the same spot through the entire pageant and look at the plastic doll in her arms and soak in all the songs that the rest of us were paraded in by age groups to sing. The littlest kids came in first, followed by the kids from each age group until we got to the "big kids" in the sixth grade. They were the oldest ones who had to do the pageant thing. Once past the sixth grade, the teenagers, who didn't think singing "Silent Night" and "Hark the Herald Angels Sing" was cool anymore, pretty much rebelled, so they got to watch like the adults. But there is one truly remarkable thing about those pageants—they packed people in. People who wouldn't have shown up at the church if it had caught fire came to see their own children or their nieces and nephews line up and sing Christmas songs. It was really fun to watch and see which kids would panic when they saw all the people in the audience. They would cry, and their parents would have to come to the front of the church and rescue them. Then there were the kids who loved every minute of it and sang at the top of their lungs and drowned everyone else out. One kid in particular was actually louder than the preacher was when he screamed. And then there was always at least one kid who felt obligated to empty his nose with one of his fingers while performing. All of this to show our love and respect for the birth of the Messiah!

For me, Christmas represented consistency. In a world of uncertainty and confusion, at least one thing held true—Christmas would be celebrated pretty much the same way each year. And of course the whole "birth of Jesus in Bethlehem's manger" story never changed, but it never seemed to bother us that we knew the whole thing from start to finish by heart. We wanted to hear it again—without changes or edits.

Through the years, my traditions have changed as I've aged, moved, and lost and added members of the family, but new practices became traditions as well. After my sister and I grew up, got married, and had our own children, we still usually went to our parents' house on Christmas Eve to open our gifts and celebrate. When we were little we celebrated most of our Christmases on Christmas Eve night because Dad had to work at the fire station on Christmas morning. The fire station is one of those places that doesn't get to close down for the holiday, and in fact, there was almost always a big fire at Christmas because people put up Christmas lights improperly or put a dried-out Christmas tree too close to a fire. We liked this tradition because it meant we got our presents the night before most of our friends did. Our parents told us that Santa made a special trip and came early to our house, and we actually believed it. I think it's one of the reasons that I didn't grow up thinking we were as poor as it turned out we were—I figured if we were important enough to warrant a special early visit from Santa, we must be a pretty big deal around Hope, Arkansas!

One of the toughest adjustments to make after Janet and I married was how to celebrate Christmas. It's difficult for every married couple; how do you combine the traditions of one family with the traditions of another? It might be easier to get Israel and the Palestinians to the peace table than to resolve some of the challenges of merging two very different family rituals into one harmonious Christmas experience.

Since my family traditions were the only ones I knew, I was pretty certain that they were the "right ones." The thought of doing Christmas differently was obviously blasphemous. If God had wanted us to have ambrosia instead of chocolate pie and crispy chocolate chip cookies as dessert, he would have written that somewhere in the Bible. The only reason explicit instructions about the chocolate pie and chocolate chip cookies were not in the Holy Writ was because everyone already knew that was the official Christmas dessert.

I did my best to hide my irritation that at Janet's house they couldn't start the Christmas dinner without ambrosia. I actually recall someone actually saying, "We can't have Christmas without the ambrosia." The heck we couldn't! I could have a lifetime of Christmases without it. I couldn't even spell it and didn't really know what it was, and when I finally learned I cared even less. As of this writing, I have been married almost thirty-six years, and I am proud to say that I have never once touched that ambrosia. I'm sure it tastes wonderful, and if it were Easter or Mother's Day, I might try it. But I have my principles!

Have you ever pondered that our traditions take on a heightened sense of certainty and become a part of the "right and wrong" way of the holiday? We tend to think that any of the activities that don't follow the script of what we're used to are not just different but wrong. Morally wrong!

I'm certain that Mary and Joseph missed having some familiar things around them the night Jesus was born. There was nothing to give them a sense of place or comfort. They were about as far removed from familiar things as they could be. Of course, they created the most important Christmas tradition themselves that night, since they were actually creating Christmas. They weren't thinking about pie or cookies, and they sure weren't thinking about ambrosia! That all sounds silly and childish when you think about what Christmas is really about, but I don't think it actually is. We establish traditions to give us connections to our past and a sense of security about the uncertainties of our future.

After both of my parents died, the idea of getting together on Christmas Eve the same old way seemed too much a painful reminder that they weren't there. So Janet and I started doing something totally different. We would attend our church's Christmas Eve service, and then my sister's family and ours would go out to eat Chinese food before gathering at our house for a brief time to observe Christmas. Now what on earth does Chinese food have to do with Christmas? Not a thing, but my dad loved Chinese food, and maybe it was our way of saying that the holiday is both a "sweet and sour" memory of the good times and the fact that our parents aren't with us anymore. Now, having Chinese food on Christmas Eve after our church's special service is as much a tradition as it once was to cut down a cedar tree, make divinity, roast pecans, and watch our dad cuss when he put his finger into the empty light sockets.

Most of our traditions aren't elaborate ones. They don't have to be. They're special because they happen every year, not because they are expensive or complicated. And they make for a very wonderful but a very simple Christmas.

6.

Crisis

My wife Janet and I thought that 1975 was going to be such a good year, but instead it was a series of crises that escalated into the most trying days of our young marriage.

Janet and I were married on May 25, 1974, when we were both just eighteen years old. At the time, I was studying theology and communications at Ouachita Baptist University and had determined that if I loaded up my class schedule each semester and took classes in the summer and in January during the "J Term," I could earn my four-year degree in two years and three months. That would save a lot of money, which was important, since I was paying for college from my earnings from working at KVRC Radio in Arkadelphia and as a part-time weekend pastor at a tiny little church in town.

We couldn't afford for both of us to be in school at the same time, so after we married, Janet suspended her education after her freshman year and went to work in a local dental office as a dental assistant. The job paid about sixty dollars a week, but between the two of us, we were able to make our forty-dollar-a-month rent payments for the little three-room duplex we occupied and eat very modestly and creatively. Whenever we cooked meat or vegetables, we took the leftovers and added them to an ever-filling Tupperware container that we kept in the freezer. When it got full of leftover hamburger meat, beans, corn, chunks of ham, onion, or whatever else hadn't been consumed, we'd thaw it, put it in a large pot, add tomato sauce, and eat what we affectionately called garbage soup. It was actually quite good and different each time we had it, and it definitely helped cut down on grocery bills. Another of our budget-stretching techniques was to take stale bread crumbs and mix them with milk to make a stuffing that we'd place in pieces of bologna and bake—we called that stuffed Arkansas round steak. To really dress it up, we'd bake it with melted cheese on top.

Life for Janet and me was simple but good. We were young, healthy, and invincible, and we had the entire world ahead of us. So we thought.

In February of 1975, Janet came home from work with pain in her back. We assumed it was the result of her standing on her feet all day, hovering over dental patients next to Dr. James Glass and Dr. Robin Glass, a married pair of dentists who practiced together in Arkadelphia. At her height, maybe it was the standing and bending over that was causing it, but what started out as just back soreness escalated into rather acute pain. Certain positions, even sitting, made it worse, and the normal home remedies like heat packs and aspirin weren't helping.

A visit to a local physician ended with a diagnosis of back strain and a prescription for some muscle relaxers, mild pain medication, and bed rest. The medicine was barely affordable, but the bed rest would have meant no work and no pay, and that combination wasn't a great option for us. We needed the money from both of our incomes to pay for Janet's medicine and our rent. Several weeks of rest when possible and medicine didn't yield any relief.

Some friends from our church recommended chiropractic treatments, so we decided to try them out. The chiropractor we went to was a wonderful man who gave it his best shot but told us after about six weeks of regular treatments that he didn't think he was helping and recommended seeing an orthopedic specialist instead. I appreciated his efforts, but, more important, his honesty. I have used chiropractors for various ailments through the years with great success, but my confidence in them actually started with the one who admitted that he couldn't help Janet instead of continuing to take our money just because he could have.

Our family physician in Arkadelphia suggested hospitalization and traction. It was not an expense we were prepared for, but fortunately we had taken out a health-insurance policy when we married because my dad insisted on it. The policy cost $17.34 a month, which was a lot of money to us then, but it turned out to be a godsend. After a week in the local hospital with no measurable improvement, Janet was referred to an orthopedic surgeon in Little Rock, about seventy-five miles from Arkadelphia. I still remember his confident, almost cocky attitude as he walked in and announced that Janet had a "textbook case" of a ruptured disc in her lower spine. "Textbook," he said. No ifs, ands, or buts, this was a ruptured disc, and it might improve on its own with extended rest or Janet might have to have surgery to repair it. Neither of the options was very appealing given that both meant more money going out of our pockets and no more coming in. I think it was during this time that I acquired my basic understanding of economics (one that I would later wish the federal government understood): When you have fewer dollars coming in, it's not possible to increase the dollars going out.

At least the doctor wasn't in too big a hurry to do surgery. Janet's pain had increased and was at times unbearable. She has a high pain threshold (unlike me, who is highly allergic to any pain and asks to be premedicated with heavy narcotics before a teeth cleaning!), and yet there were times when it was apparent that the intensity of her pain was debilitating to the point of tears. Every time she sat down or stood up was an agonizing struggle. We knew that this couldn't go on indefinitely.

By August of 1975, the orthopedic surgeon wanted to put Janet in a Little Rock hospital and try another round of traction, therapy, and medication with the understanding that if that didn't result in any improvement, surgery and disc repair would be the next course of action. Another week in an even more expensive hospital in Little Rock yielded nothing but medical bills and more lost income. The doctor told us that he would schedule surgery for her in late September. "Textbook stuff," he assured us.

Surgery was set for the third week of September. I was trying to juggle classes during what was my final semester at school, my work schedule, and getting to and from Little Rock every day to make sure Janet was okay. The day before the surgery, the doctor had scheduled a myelogram, an X-ray that involved injecting dye into the spinal area and then viewing the damaged disc to determine exactly where the incision should be.

As I sat alone in the waiting room of the radiology ward, I noticed that the test was taking longer than they had led me to believe. After a while, a nurse appeared and asked me to follow her to a small "consultation room" down the hall. Even though I was barely twenty years old, I knew that wasn't a sign that the doctor was about to give me good news. After what seemed like an eternity, the doctor finally appeared, and when he walked in, I almost didn't recognize him. His face was as white as his lab coat, and his normal proud and rather cocky attitude had been replaced by a very humble spirit. He seemed to be fumbling for words before he said, "I've canceled your wife's surgery for tomorrow. The myelogram revealed that it's not a disc after all." (So much for that textbook.) "Your wife has a tumor, and it's located within the canal of her spine and I can't operate in there. I have called in a neurosurgeon who will come and visit with you and explain what the options are."

With that, he left, and I sat there alone trying to soak in what he had just told me.

Cancer.

That's a word that twenty-year-old healthy women (or their twenty-year-old husbands) aren't supposed to be faced with, but here I was trying to come to terms with the fact that my wife had it.

Within a few hours, Dr. Thomas Fletcher, a Little Rock

neurosurgeon, walked into Janet's room at Doctors Hospital. His gentle and soft-spoken manner was comforting and reassuring, but his words cut right to our hearts. The tumor was embedded within the spinal canal and was possibly inoperable. If this was the case, there wouldn't be any treatment to cure Janet, just efforts to make the remaining days of her short life as comfortable as possible. If the tumor had not spread or could be reached, then we needed to be prepared for the likelihood that, in removing it, there would be a severing of or severe damage to the spinal cord and Janet would be paralyzed from just above the waist down for the rest of her life. Those were the two scenarios that Dr. Fletcher prepared us for, and neither gave us much hope. There in the quiet fourth-floor hospital room, it seemed that our future had been dashed on the rocks of reality.

If there was a silver lining in this cloud, my tear-filled eyes couldn't see it. I did my best to outwardly show confidence and optimism, primarily to keep Janet from giving up and also to further the façade that my faith was unshaken and firm in the face of such unexpected news.

Dr. Fletcher told us that with our approval he would schedule surgery in the next few days and would do what he could, but at the same time, he told us to understand that while we would hope for the best, he could not promise us a good outcome. He had diagnosed the tumor as a rare type of cancer that tended to reappear in other areas of the spine if there was reoccurrence. Later we came to understand that in some forms of cancer, if there is no reoccurrence after five years, the patient is considered cured, but with others a ten-year period has to pass before the patient is considered clear. Janet had the ten-year version.

The surgery was scheduled for September 29, 1975. Janet and I had been married for one year, four months, and four days. I was on schedule to complete my BA degree in December, and because of the accelerated pace at which I had worked on my degree, the fall semester of 1975 turned out to be my lightest of all. In fact, I only had to complete eight academic hours to fulfill my degree requirements, and six of those were for a class that I was taking on Tuesday and Thursday nights, so that meant that by sheer Providence, I would have more free time than usual to take care of my sick young wife.

Of course, just when you don't think things can get worse, they usually do. While I was in the hospital room visiting Janet, someone broke into my car in broad daylight in the hospital parking lot and stole a CB radio and a little briefcase that contained a Bible, some college textbooks, and some class notes from a theology course I was taking. While I could see the irony in the thief opening the briefcase and finding a Bible and class notes for a course in biblical studies, the thought that a thief who was probably wealthier than me at that moment would break into *my* car just about did me in. I truly wondered if God had moved and left no forwarding address. If He was answering my prayers, He was doing it on a different frequency than the one I was monitoring, and I had to wonder about the why of it all.

Janet had had to leave her job weeks earlier due to the back problems, and we had been forced to make do without her income. On top of that, the church where I worked part time was so small and so broke that, in the very midst of Janet's health crisis, they had had to stop paying me for six weeks because they had run out of money.

In addition to my two jobs, and my new job taking care of Janet, I wrote a weekly column for a Baptist newspaper published in Arkansas. I had been doing this since my junior year of high school, and within the circle of churches affiliated with the Baptist Missionary Association of Arkansas (a much smaller denomination than Southern Baptists), I had earned some name recognition. As word spread of the situation with Janet, I received some stunning correspondence from people who pointedly told me that the calamities we were experiencing were surely "God's punishment" for some untold evil one or both of us had committed. How anyone could be both that stupid and that cold-hearted in the name of Jesus escapes me even now.

But just as some used the brokenness of our lives and spirits like crushed gravel to walk upon, others were incredibly compassionate, and we were overwhelmed with the kindnesses of both our dear friends and total strangers.

In addition to the nasty notes of condemnation, the mail brought notes of encouragement, often with small amounts of money inside from a Sunday-school class in some church we'd never heard of or from some dear, sweet family who had been through something similar and were now offering their encouragement to us. Most of the gifts we received were between five and twenty-five dollars, but at a time when our income had disappeared and our expenses had increased dramatically, we had just enough to make it. My college roommate, Rick

Caldwell, was especially instrumental in helping. His dad, a wealthy oil and gas distributor and cattle rancher, helped pay some of the medical bills that our insurance didn't cover and even got some of his friends to join him. It was humbling to have so many people show their kindness to us, but it changed our perspective on the way we lived. Through the years, Janet and I have quietly but regularly given gifts large and small to people we learned were facing a crisis. In some cases, they were people we knew, but in other cases, they were total strangers we'd read about or met as we went about our daily routines.

The surgery was scheduled for 7:00 A.M., and we had been told that it could last eight hours or more, so we were prepared for a long wait. Janet's mother, Pat, drove up from Hope to be there. She brought some knitting to work on to keep her mind occupied for what we assumed would be a very long, tedious, and exhausting day. Dr. Fletcher had explained that his likely course of action was to make the incision in the lower back around lumbar vertebrae five and six, use a surgical microscope to see how embedded the tumor was inside the spinal canal, and then attempt to remove it by scraping it away from the spinal cord. The degree to which it had attached itself to the spinal cord would determine the permanent damage that would be done to save her life or would indicate that the tumor was inoperable, in which case it was only a matter of time before her body could no longer fight off the aggressive invader.

At about 9:30 in the morning, I was standing in the hall near the surgical waiting room talking with a visitor who had dropped by to offer prayers and encouragement when I thought I saw Dr. Fletcher walking toward me down the long hallway.

As he got closer, I noticed that not only was it definitely Dr. Fletcher, but he wasn't wearing his surgical scrubs and had already changed into a suit and tie as if heading to his office. The fact that we had not received any indication of the progress of the surgery nor had any update from a nurse or other hospital personnel added to the size of the lump in my throat as he approached and asked to visit privately with Janet's mother and me. The only thing I could think was that either Janet hadn't made it through the surgery or that Dr. Fletcher had opened her up, looked at the situation, and simply closed her back up. I tried to brace myself for horrible news. The worried look on my mother-in-law's face quickly gave way to tears as she too realized the news that she was likely about to hear.

Dr. Fletcher then calmly and gently told us that when he had gotten to the tumor, expecting it to be firmly attached or wrapped in the spinal cord, he had started the extraction and it had simply dislodged. He said he was surprised, but he had been able to remove the four- or five-inch elongated tumor that had grown inside the bony structure of her spine. I'll never forget him saying, "I think you guys had a lot of people praying for her . . . and me."

He was right.

The next few hours were tense and seemed to last forever. While the tumor had dislodged and been removed, only time would tell if there had been any permanent damage to the spinal cord and with it, a lifetime of paralysis. After Janet was brought out of the ICU and into her room, we waited and watched to see if there was movement in her legs—that would be the sign that she had not experienced irreversible damage.

She was heavily sedated, and we were told that it would be a while before the anesthetic wore off enough for her to regain movement. It was almost 4:00 P.M. when the stillness of the room was interrupted by the sudden movement of her feet under the covers. Everyone in the room wept with joy at a simple but very reassuring movement that ordinarily we would have taken for granted. We wouldn't take anything for granted after that.

As relieved as we were that the worst seemed to be over, the postoperative period brought its own challenges. Due to the nature of the tumor, Dr. Fletcher advised that Janet undergo six weeks of intense radiation therapy to eradicate any cancer cells that the surgery might have missed. Other than the normal downside to radiation (especially in 1975, when some of the procedures were primitive by today's standards), we were warned that the location of the radiation in the lower part of her back and pelvis would likely mean that the inevitable damage done to her ovaries would make having children impossible. This was devastating news, naturally, but in the past few months, we had learned to live with what we had now, not what we hoped might happen in the future. Without the radiation we knew there might not be a future.

After a week in the hospital recovering, Janet was ready to come home to our little duplex in Arkadelphia. It consisted of two rooms, a living room and a tiny bedroom, plus a small kitchen and a bathroom that was so small that there was barely room to stand sideways between the tub and the sink and toilet. I rented a hospital bed from a local medical supply store and set it up in the living room. It pretty much took up the entire room, but it was a necessary inconvenience for the next several weeks, since Janet would have limited mobility and would need a bar over the bed to be able to lift herself so she could have her sheets changed or move the bedpan. She had to be brought back home in an ambulance because she wasn't able to walk yet. We had a couple of weeks at home for her to start the recovery process before she would start the radiation therapy.

I piled pillows, blankets, and an old camping mattress in the backseat of the car so she could lie down for the drive to and from Little Rock each day once the radiation got under way. This meant leaving the apartment around five fifteen each morning for the seventy-five-mile trip each way. We would arrive a little after seven o'clock, and she would have her treatment. The actual radiation lasted only about four minutes each day, but the preparation took about forty-five minutes. Shortly after eight o'clock, we'd be on our way back to Arkadelphia. I'd help her out of the car, partially carry her to the house, and get her settled back in the hospital bed, and then it would be time for me to head off to work or to class. I'd check in through the day before returning home to make dinner and help her get to sleep, and then I'd study until I fell asleep and the next morning's alarm went off at four thirty for us to get up and do it all again.

Five days a week for six straight weeks we made the trip. By the time we had finished, Janet had regained the ability to walk unassisted, which in itself was progress. It was early December when the radiation treatments ended and so did my course requirements for my degree. For months, we had planned on moving to Fort Worth, Texas, following my graduation so I could enroll at Southwestern Baptist Theological Seminary, where I hoped to further prepare for what I thought was a future in some form of Christian broadcasting, either radio or television or both. We had feared that all of those plans might have to be delayed, but Janet seemed strong enough to make the move, and frankly, we decided that it was just as easy to be broke and struggling through school in Fort Worth as to be broke and not even going to school in Arkansas. I applied, was accepted, and then received notice that we had been accepted for seminary-owned housing in Fort Worth. The letter said that we'd be living in a two-bedroom house near the campus and the rent would be seventy-five dollars a month. Since our little duplex was forty dollars a month, we were thinking that a two-bedroom house that cost almost twice as much must be some nice place.

My dad helped us move, which wasn't too difficult since we were able to put everything we owned in our car and a small U-Haul trailer, which my dad pulled behind his truck. The move to Fort Worth would be a new beginning and an opportunity to close what had been an instructive but painful chapter in our lives. We would be moving just about a week before Christmas, so this would be the first Christmas since Janet's cancer, and for both of us it was the farthest we'd ever lived from our families. To us, Fort Worth was the "big city," since the biggest place we'd ever lived had been Arkadelphia with about ten thousand people in the entire town.

We carefully followed the instructions and map to get to our new house, which we imagined would have two decent-sized bedrooms with closets, hopefully two bathrooms, a living room, and a kitchen, with maybe a porch and a street with trees and a sidewalk. In our minds, we must have been thinking *Leave It to Beaver* meets *Mayberry.*

When we pulled in to the address, we couldn't help it. We both literally started laughing out loud. We had to, because crying wouldn't have helped and at this stage of our lives, we didn't care what kind of house we lived in as long as we were living. So we laughed when we saw that our "two-bedroom" house on Warren Street behind the seminary campus was sitting just off the single-lane, dead-end street and directly in front of the Katy Railroad tracks, which were at best forty yards from the back door. And the back door was *really* close to the front door, since the entire house couldn't have occupied more than five hundred square feet. The "two bedrooms" were more the size of one with a hastily placed wall stuck in the middle to create another. There was one bathroom, which made the one in our old house look like a palace! The "living room" was barely an entryway to the kitchen, which was about the size of a Pullman kitchen. The floors were made of concrete covered with very cheap linoleum that was coming up in several places. One of our friends came to see us shortly after we moved in and proclaimed it "the Winnebago." That would have been an insult to Winnebago, because even a medium-sized Winnebago is more spacious and far more welcoming than our new "house." If the little rectangular house had had wheels, it would have truly looked like a Winnebago with a slightly pitched roof. But it was home and the rent was cheap, and I could walk or ride a bicycle to campus each day.

That year had been a challenge to our finances, our families, our friends, and our faith. There were times when I questioned why God would allow such an experience to befall us. "Here we are, trying to be decent people and living our lives by believing in *You*, God," I would pray. "Why is this happening to us?" It seemed like the answer was "Why not you? Are you too good to experience the hardships that the rest of the world has to live through?"

In time, the answers would get clearer. When I served as a pastor in Pine Bluff, Arkansas, a few years later, I often entered the hospital room of a family who had received a similar little visit down the hall from a doctor who had uttered the same word I had heard a few years earlier—cancer. I could honestly say to them, "I do know how you feel," and it mattered that I was not just talking about something abstract but speaking from the perspective of having been confronted with all the fears one has when getting that diagnosis. This happened almost every week of my time as a pastor.

We settled in to our little "Winnebago," and I prepared to start classes in January while diligently looking for a way to make enough money to pay our rent and my tuition.

By then it was only a few days before Christmas—our first one as "refugees from Arkansas." We had decided to go back to Hope for Christmas Day, even though the trip would be tough on Janet.

The year had been one that had tested us to our core. We had faced down death and disability and survived. I had often prayed that we would experience a sudden and dramatic "miracle" and fully expected on several occasions to walk into the hospital and hear that she had been instantly and supernaturally healed to the complete surprise of the doctors. That never happened. Had it happened, we would have loved it. I could already hear in my mind the powerful testimony we could give about faith and the miracle on the other end of the experience. But it would have been a story that was so grand and so out of the ordinary that most people couldn't have related to it. If the listeners facing cancer didn't have the same outcome, such a testimony likely would have discouraged them into believing that something was wrong with them.

We learned more from taking the long trail instead of the shortcut and more often than not found that having experienced it, we had credibility to bring encouragement to others who had as many valleys as mountaintops.

The Christmas of 1975 was perhaps our simplest ever. Neither of us had money to buy anything for the other that year, but neither of us wanted any "thing" anyway. That year, we celebrated something far greater than a gift that could be wrapped and placed under the tree. Christmas often was the anticipation of what we were going to eat or what gifts we would receive or what kind of Christmas lights we would see. Something was dramatically different about this Christmas. We had made it to Christmas, and life and hope were all that we wanted. The lights were just as bright and the Christmas food was just as good, but it was the first Christmas ever that no gift at all could have equaled the one we cherished most. We celebrated life itself, and it was a pretty good reminder of what really matters in life. No one openly talked about death or cancer, but the expressions and subtle comments my family members made that day proved that everyone realized that, but for the grace of

God, Janet might not have been with us that Christmas. I honestly don't remember a thing either of us received that year in the way of gifts, but nothing would have overshadowed the gift we truly cherished—her being alive.

That Christmas we learned that God's greatest gift to us is not to remove us from crisis, but to walk through crisis with us. He does not do us a favor by taking us out of all the trials and tribulations of life, but strengthens us by giving us the grace to get through them and emerge on the other side having realized that what we thought we couldn't endure we in fact just did. How often do we ask for the gift of escape from a problem and instead it seems to escalate? When we want Christmas to represent the easy path and the glittery gifts, we fail to understand that the real message of the Messiah is that the first Christmas was the opposite of easy. It was more about long stretches of darkness and loneliness, instead of the stunning stars that were eventually seen in the night sky. Before the angels sang and the shepherds saw stars, a scared couple fumbled their way around a strange town and endured pain and humiliation. True faith is forged in the furnace, not the showroom.

It might have been our simplest Christmas ever. We had nothing but family, our traditions, and each other. But as it turned out, those simple things were the best things, and we will always remember 1975 because we celebrated the simplest but most precious gift of all—the gift of life.

7.

Hope

By the end of the year, Janet and I were glad to get 1975 behind us. A year of progressively worse struggles and downward spirals had left us to believe that we would surely have a better Christmas the next year. We weren't disappointed!

When we got back to Fort Worth after the brief Christmas visit to our families in Hope, it was like starting all over again. We lived in a new place in a new town, and I was starting graduate school in a new environment. Janet was getting stronger and healthier each day, and soon we would both start looking for new jobs.

We had learned during the previous year just how insignificant material things really are in the hierarchy of values. When you aren't sure if you're going to be alive in a few months, having "things" suddenly doesn't seem so important. Janet and I had started our marriage with pretty much nothing, and before we had even reached our second anniversary, we had reduced that by quite a bit! But after the crisis we had just been through, we didn't seem to mind not having a lot of "stuff." Having next to nothing can be a blessing in that it lets you fully appreciate what little you do have, and more important, it makes you grateful that you still have the *one thing* that does matter—life itself.

Janet found a job as a dental assistant for a dentist whose office was very near our house and the seminary. It was a perfect job for her, and while the pay wasn't great, it was adequate, and the dentist, Dr. Harold Cohen, was very good to her. He had been an army dentist for several years before going into private practice, and in many ways he still had the military mind-set of how to run things. Janet loved working for him, and although the money was critical for us, her ability to work again was a true blessing in that it affirmed just how alive she was. In a strange way, coming so close to death really brings you closer to life. Those who have stood in the shadow of death quickly learn to appreciate the simple things that remind them, "You are alive." You realize that a job is more than employment; it's a sign of *hope* and optimism that you are going to be around a while and that there is a future being planned with you in it.

I had come to Fort Worth with the anticipation of working for a Christian ministry that had planned on hiring me, but by the time I arrived, the finances of the organization were strained and it was unable to offer me a job. That forced me to hit the streets looking for something—anything—so we could survive. I had completed my training and clinical work to be an EMT and applied at several ambulance services and emergency rooms, but either they weren't hiring or I didn't have enough experience to work in the "big city." I applied for every job I could find, including working on freight docks and waiting tables in restaurants, and was constantly turned away with the worst excuse ever—"You're overqualified." Yes, I was a college graduate who had completed a four-year degree in just over two years and graduated magna cum laude, and yes, I didn't really *want* to wait tables or ask customers, "Would you like fries or a baked potato?" as a career, but that didn't mean I wasn't willing to work hard. Looking for a job can be humbling. Mustering the courage to ask for the interview and just being told no makes a person feel like a leper. I can fully understand how easy it would be for a person to get utterly frustrated and simply quit looking for a job because the wounds of the process are so painful and the process can be so demeaning. I finally realized that I was trying to get someone to hire me for something I was not likely to do long term because it was clearly not my career goal. Why would someone hire me to wait tables, load freight, or stabilize a victim of a car wreck when it was apparent that I didn't really plan on doing that for the rest of my life?

But there was something I had done since I was fourteen years old and still enjoyed very much—radio. The likelihood I would be hired to be a DJ or a sportscaster in a major market was about zero, but I could freelance and write, produce, and do voice spots. And so I set out to find possible clients. I had some contacts with some megachurches and large Christian organizations and offered to do some spots at no cost that they could then buy if they liked them and wanted to use them. Fortunately for me, they did like them and did pay for them and even recommended me to some other organizations. I was picking up enough work, and between Janet and me, we could cover our rent. Just barely, but we could do it.

If you are thinking these were our worst days, think again. In so many ways, they were our best. We had escaped a galloping terror just months earlier, and if there's one good thing about hitting bottom it's that you know that there's nowhere to go but up. Having been there, you know what it feels like; it's much easier to believe that things are going to get better and that you can handle anything life throws at you.

To save money, Janet and I ate peanut-butter-and-jelly sandwiches and canned soup virtually every day. It was cheap and there was no waste. We varied the flavor of the soup to give ourselves some variety, and grocery shopping was easy. Every Tuesday, a little taco stand not far from our house sold tacos for twenty-five cents each, and we'd splurge and spend fifty cents to treat ourselves to a dinner "out." We can laugh about it now, but that was a big treat for us then.

For my new job, I bought a suit at a factory outlet for $12.50. It was a blue polyester knit suit with patterns on the pocket. I can only pray that no one finds photos of me wearing that hideous thing, but I needed at least one suit for the occasions on which I was invited to speak in a church or do something "important." I had a pair of black dress shoes that I wore with the suit, and for everyday wear, I had an old pair of brown casual shoes with rubber soles that were more comfortable for walking back and forth to class. About halfway through the semester, the sole of one of these shoes separated from the rest of the shoe, and one of the guys in my Greek class made fun of me because he thought I was wearing them to be cool and to show my rebellious and independent streak. I laughed along with him, not wanting him to know that I wasn't wearing worn-out shoes to make some kind of statement. It was simply all I had.

I started seminary as a twenty-year-old. The average age of the other students in my classes was thirty, as seminary tended to attract older students who had started a career of one kind only to decide later to pursue a theology degree and do full-time Christian ministry or mission work. As best I could tell, I was the youngest student in any of my classes. Most of the "younger" guys were at least twenty-two or twenty-three, and many were in their forties or even fifties. I looked like a kid compared to them.

Southwestern was at the time the largest Christian seminary in the world, with over 4,000 students on campus. It touted itself as the largest institution in history that provided full-time training for Christian ministry. That meant most of the classes were large, with as many as 110 students packed into a single lecture hall. I was way too timid to try to make myself stand out. I felt like such a small and insignificant part of what was going on there, but I also felt incredibly privileged just to be there.

The academic environment was challenging, but the spirit of the classes was more like that at evangelistic meetings because the professors taught with such passion and fire, not simply reading the yellowed pages of lecture notes prepared a generation earlier. To this day, I recall the glisten in the eyes of Dr. William Tolar as he extolled the power of archaeology in helping to validate the veracity of the Bible; the flame in the voice of Dr. Roy Fish as he urged us to find a way to translate faith into a transferable gift to others through evangelism; and the enthusiasm of Dr. Thomas Urrey (known as "Hurry Urrey" because of the speed at which he expected his students to master the intricacies of the Koine Greek language of the New Testament), who took a dead language (Koine Greek is no longer a spoken language) and brought it to life with his enthusiasm about its precision to give us clarity in the scripture. Even in church history class Dr. William Estep had me on the edge of my seat as he told the narratives.

I looked forward to every day at school, even though I always felt a bit like a fish out of water. I was so much younger than my classmates, I wasn't a "somebody," and my fashion choices were more warehouse than Wall Street, but being provided a daily dose of hope and optimism helped me overlook these details. The daily chapel services were packed, and each day, my heart was stirred with messages of challenge to "change the world." It hardly seemed like a twenty-year-old wearing shoes with big holes in them was in a position to change a lightbulb, much less the world, but numerous cells of vision were implanted into my spiritual and intellectual consciousness each day, and now that those days of facing Janet's cancer seemed further away than ever, the future seemed a journey worth taking.

Janet and I had pretty much established our routine by now. During the week, I walked or rode a bicycle to class and she drove to the dental office for work. At lunch, we would both make the short trip to the Winnebago-sized house, where we would have a peanut-butter sandwich and share a can of soup. Then I'd go back to class and then come home to start studying and trying to peddle some of my radio spots. Sundays were, of course, for church, but on Saturdays we tried to dedicate at least half a day to exploring Fort Worth by driving through a section of the city and getting acquainted with it. On one Saturday, we drove to the far western side of the city to the gates of Carswell Air Force Base, which at the time was one of our nation's major bases in the Strategic Air Command. Since we were both from small towns, one of the things that captivated us was the inspiring and majestic sight of the ever-present B-52 bombers flying in and out of Carswell twenty-four hours a day. The closer one got to the base, the more massive those jets became. They were an ominous sight with their one-of-a-kind wing-over-fuselage look and their massive engines ready to fly them literally around the world and back with a nuclear bomb aboard, prepared to face any threat that came their way.

We still laugh with embarrassment when we tell our friends about the day we drove right up to the gates of Carswell and, when the sharply dressed sentinel snapped at us and asked what we wanted, told him, "We just wanted to look around and see the planes." Judging from the stunned look on his face, he must have thought we were bozos. "Sir," he said, "this is a SAC base. No visitors are allowed on these premises."

Hey, we didn't know. We figured they'd love to have us come and look around and be proud of what our tax dollars were supporting. But I guess they figured we could be equally proud watching from *outside* the gates.

Janet's physical condition continued to improve as she regained strength, stamina, and her ability to walk and move without the limitations that the "year from hell" had presented.

We had nothing but the used and borrowed furniture that occupied our little "two-bedroom" house, but we had each other and were enjoying life.

We became good friends with several other couples from our church, a few of whom were also in seminary and just as poor as we were. Our friends Jerry and Glenda Woods lived just blocks from us in seminary housing, and to save gas, we would take turns driving to the Hulen Street Baptist Church, where we all attended. Jerry and Glenda were from Tennessee, so they "spoke Southern," and neither of them had come from wealthy or storied families, so we had much in common. Jerry was preparing to be a pastor, and I was still hoping to work in some form of Christian broadcasting. We had a lot in common, but one big difference between us was that they had a young son. Since we knew that, due to Janet's radiation, we weren't likely to ever be able to have children of our own, we delighted in their two-year-old, Jeremy. We enjoyed watching him grow and sharing milestones in his development. He was a well-behaved and content child, and Janet would usually sit in the backseat with Glenda and they would play with Jeremy, who sat in a car seat between them. Jerry and I would sit in the front and discuss the issues of the day and how we would handle them if someone would just put us in charge.

I could tell that Janet enjoyed those trips playing and talking with the baby, and there were times I sensed how tough it must be wondering what it would be like to have the children cancer and radiation had stolen from her. If she was distraught over it, she never let on, and we never spoke about it; it was a part of our lives we simply had to accept. On Good Friday of 1976, I made my way home for lunch as I did every day. Janet had arrived before me and already had the peanut-butter-and-jelly sandwich ready and the soup all warmed up. But on the table was an Easter basket, which I thought a bit strange since we were both adults and hardly planned on going on an Easter egg hunt. She had the most apprehensive look on her face but urged me to look in the basket. She had put the typical plastic grass in the bottom and a few plastic eggs, one of which was marked with my name on it. Not one to wait on opening things, I naturally picked it up and opened it. A note inside the egg said, "By next Easter, we'll need the basket for our own little baby's first Easter." That seemed strange. What baby? We couldn't have one, we had been told, so this note could mean only one of three things: (1) Janet wanted to adopt a baby and figured that an impoverished couple who worked and went to school and had no tangible assets would be approved for adoption. (Delusional!); (2) She planned on our kidnapping someone else's child à la the movie *Raising Arizona* and needed psychiatric help immediately; (3) The doctors had been wrong.

At that moment, I was afraid to say something really stupid and get excited that she was actually pregnant only to find out she was talking about getting a puppy. Then she would get depressed and angry because I "didn't really want the puppy" or she thought I was "unhappy in the marriage because we couldn't have kids."

I asked the questions slowly and deliberately. Are you pregnant? How do you know? Have you been to a doctor to know this? Which one? Are you sure?

She had been having some strange feelings and some nausea

and thinking that it was a holdover from the radiation, so she had decided to ask a doctor about it. The seminary had a clinic on campus, and a family-health physician would come over a couple of days a week to see students. She had gone there and after describing the symptoms was administered a pregnancy test. It was positive. She explained that something must be wrong as pregnancy wasn't possible. Another test said the same thing. A few phone calls between doctors in Fort Worth and Little Rock seemed to have everyone arriving at the same conclusion.

The good news—she *was* pregnant. This alone was pretty much a miracle because we had given up the hope of ever having a child of our own.

The bad news—while the pregnancy was indeed surprising, there was immediate concern that Janet might not be able to carry the child to term, and there was an even greater likelihood that, if she could carry the child to term, the baby would be at risk for birth defects due to the radiation.

The news brought hope tempered by reality, but for me the mere fact that Janet was pregnant was all that mattered. I was ecstatic. At that moment, I wasn't thinking about how we would possibly survive the cost of a birth, taking care of a baby, and losing one of the two paltry incomes we had. But somehow I knew the human race had survived with couples who had less than we did and far more obstacles in front of them. Even that couple in Bethlehem so long ago faced tougher odds than we did, so I knew that we could worry about our troubles later. We had received one miracle; now we would just have to start praying for a few more.

My exuberance over the thought of a baby was hard to contain. It was April, and the baby wasn't due until December, which meant that her pregnancy was in the earliest stages, and the doctors warned us that the first three months were critical to make sure that the development was normal and that Janet didn't miscarry. For that reason, we decided that we would wait a few months to tell our families so they wouldn't get their hopes up and wouldn't have to worry about us as much. Of course, keeping this to ourselves was difficult because news like that is tailor made to shout, not hide. But we kept mum.

As we started thinking about the many changes headed our way, we had to start getting very practical. The "Winnebago" by the train tracks barely accommodated us, and we knew we needed to think about moving into a bigger place. We also needed to figure out how we were going to afford another family member.

God watches after little kids and idiots, so I guess he did double duty to watch out for the little kid that Janet was carrying and the idiots who were about to become parents. During one of my radio-spot-recording gigs, it turned out that Gordon Waller, who produced spots for James Robison's Evangelistic Association, was in the studio I was using and heard the spots. He learned that I was a seminary student and asked me if I would like to audition to do spots for the Robison organization. The person they currently used lived somewhere on the East Coast, and the organization thought it would be better to use someone who lived locally and could record on short notice. Keep in mind that this was before the days of MP3 files and the Internet. In fact, it was even before most businesses had fax machines. (And I'm not talking about the modern fax machine but its predecessor, in which an 8½ × 11–inch original document was placed on a round tube and then a telephone handset was set into a cradle and a call placed to another identical machine. At the other end, a tissue-thin thermograph paper would have the grainiest of images burned into it after three to six minutes.)

The opportunity to be the voice of the James Robison Crusade radio spots was a huge deal for me, and a month after I did the first one I was asked to work at their headquarters every day after class doing spots, buying ads, writing things for the organization, and doing any other duties for the in-house advertising agency that worked on their crusades, television show, and magazine. It was high cotton for a kid like me to work at a place like this, and it meant a steady and much larger income. We weren't rich by any means, but we had enough to make it.

By Father's Day of that year, Janet was in the third month of her pregnancy, and we knew that we were going to have to break the news to our family and friends before Janet started showing. We were of course giddy with excitement to get back to Hope that weekend and tell both her mother, Pat, and my parents. Her mother's initial reaction was more worry than excitement. It took a while for her to quit thinking about the year behind us and start thinking about the year in front of us. She of course was happy over the announcement, but her joy was tempered by her anxiety that it might put too much stress on her daughter, who had been through a tough year.

For my parents, it would be the first grandchild, and there was some concern about Janet's health, but mostly they were visibly excited. Of course, my parents the pragmatists were instantly concerned about how on earth we could possibly afford a child. I'm not sure my response, "The Lord will provide," was quite what they wanted to hear. I think they were hoping for a big salary increase on my part. The Lord's version would have to suffice for now.

Janet and I found another house to rent not far from the seminary, but this one was privately owned by a former seminary student who rented it out. The rent was ninety dollars a month, but the house was a real two-bedroom house and even had a fenced-in backyard. It wasn't great, but it was just what we would need. The move wasn't that difficult since it was only a few blocks and we didn't have a lot of stuff—a kitchen table with four chairs that my dad had gotten secondhand from people who had abandoned them in an apartment, bedroom furniture that had been salvaged from my parents' house, and an old couch that my parents were going to get rid of when they got a new one. Janet's mother gave us a wooden rocking chair and we later bought a hide-a-bed sofa on sale at a furniture dealer in Fort Worth that we would use if parents or friends came to stay to help with the baby. Our next-door neighbor, Mark Baber, was a fellow seminary student who had been a classmate of mine at Ouachita, and the two of us went in together to buy a used lawn mower for ten dollars so that we could take turns using it to mow our lawns. On the other side of us lived two couples—one married, one not—who we were pretty sure were drug dealers, seeing as they actually kept a chair on their rooftop where one of them sat most of the night, we presumed to guard their stash. All I know is that we got along with them just fine and never worried about security because one of them was keeping watch all night. They also provided occasional entertainment of the soap opera kind when the unmarried female would get angry at her live-in boyfriend and throw all of his stuff in the front yard. The episodes were fully enriched with lively dialogue and mystery but always ended just like a TV show, with things getting resolved, an emotional reunion, and all the stuff going back into the house.

While we had enough money to pay the rent, we knew that having a baby was going to mean other costs, like diapers. Disposable diapers were out of the question due to cost, so we were forced to use cloth diapers, which cost less since they could be reused. But washing diapers would mean extra work if we had to make weekly trips to the coin-operated Laundromat as we had done all through our marriage. The house had a space and hookup for a washer and dryer, and we knew that if we had those appliances, we could save not only money but also time. It would also be much safer for Janet than having to traipse off to the laundry with a newborn. Problem was, how would we ever afford a washer and a dryer?

That's when I decided to sell the guitars I told you about in chapter 2—a 1967 Gretsch Tennessean six-string electric guitar and a 1968 Fender Jazz Bass—plus a Gibson amplifier for the Gretsch and a Kustom bass amp for the Fender. Without really discussing it with Janet, because I knew she would sell one of her kidneys if it meant I could hang on to those guitars, I placed an ad in the local free shopper, a newspaper left on racks around town that contained mostly classified ads. Soon after the paper hit the newsstands, a man and his son called and asked to come see the guitars. They were both musicians in their local Pentecostal church band and were looking for nicer instruments than they had. These were nice enough for George Harrison and Paul McCartney, so they were certainly adequate for a Texas church band!

They made an offer on the spot that was within twenty-five dollars of my asking price. I gulped and realized that I was about to sell things I valued more than any other material possessions I had ever owned. But then I thought about my bigger and more pressing responsibility as a husband and a father-to-be and said, "Okay, it's a deal." The man reached into his wallet and counted out the money in cash. I couldn't watch and had to turn away as the excited man and his twenty-something son loaded what had once been the apples of my eye into their car and drove off.

I had no second thoughts about my decision, but that night I realized that from that point onward my life would never be quite the same. Starting then, my commitment to my wife and child would come first, and my old priorities would slip away. It would be exactly twenty years before I owned a bass guitar again.

We bought the washer and dryer, and then as the due date drew closer, we tried to ready the part of the little bedroom that would be set aside for the "nursery." We found a used baby crib for ten dollars at a used furniture store and a used playpen for five dollars at a garage sale. We were getting ready!

These were the days before ultrasounds, so the only clue we had as to the gender of our baby was our doctor's speculation, and he was adamant that we were going to have a girl. He was a wonderful physician and was highly regarded in the field. He was semiretired and only worked at the seminary medical clinic as a sort of Christian mission because he knew that most of the seminary students were only a couple of meals away from starving. He attended one of the local Southern Baptist churches, and his caring for the students and their families was as much a gift as any medical practice, because he certainly wasn't making any money from us!

His name was Dr. David Pillow, and he reminded us of Marcus Welby, M.D., in both manner and looks. Dr. Pillow's gentle and reassuring manner was just what we needed. He seemed especially sensitive to Janet's previous medical history and knew how anxious we were over every little ache and pain. In the interest of full disclosure, I was a much bigger handful than Janet. She seemed to regard this entire process as a mother would—an affirmation of her womanhood and instincts. I, on the other hand, was terrified that we would do something terribly wrong and always walked into the appointments for the prenatal checkups with a long list of questions. If we had been charged by the question, I would have needed to find some more guitars to sell!

I'll never forget the day that, in a moment of true candor and wisdom, Dr. Pillow interrupted one of my interrogations and said, "I need to remind you of something. Childbirth is not a disease. Your wife isn't sick. She is going to have a baby—not another tumor. She is simply doing what God created her with the capacity to do, and it's been done for thousands of years without doctors and hospitals and medical equipment. She will be fine and doesn't really even need me for this to work. I'm not there to make it happen, just to make sure that what she does naturally is as comfortable as possible."

I needed that. I probably really needed a slap on the face, but he was too nice for that.

The baby was due on December 11, 1976. Dr. Pillow told us that since this was our first child, it would probably arrive late. He guessed it might even arrive two weeks after the original date—on Christmas Day.

It was good to have a doctor who exuded confidence and certainty. So there we had it. We were going to have our little girl on Christmas Day—two weeks after she was due. We were prepared for that. And so was he. In fact, we were so confident that Dr. Pillow planned his annual deer hunt the week of Thanksgiving so he could be sure to be around for the birth.

Everyone was totally in sync with the plan. That is, everyone except the baby.

Janet and I planned to forego a Thanksgiving trip to Arkansas to spare Janet the long car ride. A friend from church called and offered us two tickets to the Dallas Cowboys football game on Thanksgiving Day. He knew that we had a few weeks before the baby came and it might be our last chance for an outing. Neither of us had ever been to a Dallas Cowboys game, even though we were both big fans, so how could we say no? I would take my wife, now eight months pregnant, to the Thanksgiving Day game. Dr. Pillow was deer hunting, and we still had two to four weeks before the baby would arrive.

The game was great, and though tired, Janet handled the experience well. She was probably an even bigger Dallas fan than I was, and I think if she had gone into labor in the stands, we still would have sat through the entire game.

We took things pretty easy on the Friday and Saturday of

Thanksgiving weekend, and of course we talked on the phone to our families and apologized for not being able to be home for the holiday.

Early Sunday morning, Janet woke me up and said she didn't feel well. She thought that maybe the ballgame had overdone it a bit. It was cold that day—twenty-two degrees, a record low for Fort Worth on November 28. Being the ever-vigilant dad-to-be, I asked Janet if she thought she was going into labor. She was adamant that it couldn't be that. First, it was two weeks before the original due date and Dr. Pillow had said the baby would probably be late, not early. Second, Dr. Pillow was still deer hunting, and how could she possibly have the baby with him off God-knows-where in the woods trying to shoot a deer?

By 7:00 A.M., her symptoms sounded a lot like labor to me, but she assured me that it was probably "false labor," and she didn't want to drive to the hospital only to look like an idiot and be sent home. We finally agreed to call the hospital, and after we described the symptoms, we were instructed to head to the hospital. Janet asked if Dr. Pillow would be there and was told that he wouldn't be available, but not to worry because someone was on call for him and would be in to check her out by the time we arrived. That didn't go over too well. A total stranger taking over for Marcus Welby?! And it probably wasn't going to be James Brolin, either. (If you understand the whole Marcus Welby/James Brolin reference, that just means you're as old as dirt like I am now!)

On this bitterly cold day, I tried to warm up the car and convince a reluctant and expectant wife that we couldn't wait until Dr. Pillow came back from the deer hunt in a couple of days. We needed to go *now.*

The small Glenview Hospital (which is now a nursing home) was on the opposite side of Fort Worth but was a nice neighborhood-type hospital that Dr. Pillow liked. It was about a thirty-minute drive ordinarily, but on that Sunday morning, we made the trip in about twenty minutes. I only confess this now, as I feel certain that the statute of limitations on speeding violations in Texas has long since passed.

We checked into the hospital a little after nine that morning, and at 3:04 P.M., November 28, 1976, we saw God's gift of hope to a young mother who a year before was fighting for her life. Now she was *giving* life in the form of a 5-pound, 15¼-ounce, 19-inch-long, redheaded baby *boy.* The doctor had guessed wrong not only about *when* the baby was coming but also about *who* it would be. That little girl he was so certain we would have was in fact a little boy whom we named John Mark. John means "God's beloved" or "God's gift" and Mark means "protector." He was surely God's beloved gift, and we hoped he would be a protector of the miracle that he was to us.

Our Christmas girl turned out to be a Thanksgiving boy, but this meant that less than four weeks later, we took our new son home to Arkansas at Christmas to see his grandparents, his uncles and aunts, and a lot of other people who just wanted to see this little guy who had surprised us all.

For the trip home, a friend of ours gave us a little red and white Santa hat for John Mark. It was as tiny as he was, but he looked priceless in his Christmas outfit. That year, instead of the usual presents under the tree for each other, Janet and I put

John Mark in his little plastic baby carrier and placed him, wearing his Christmas cap, under the tree. We took his picture and decided that he was our gift to each other that year. Nothing else could have come close.

That was the only year that little Christmas hat fit on John Mark's ever-growing head, but every year when we put up our family Christmas tree, we don't top it with the typical star or angel. Not that there's anything wrong with those traditional tree toppers, but we top our tree with that little red Santa hat that did a lot more than simply crown the dome of our month-old baby boy on his first Christmas. It serves as a reminder of how out of the depths of despair and the shadow of death can spring hope and expectancy and, ultimately, affirmation. Affirmation that the past is truly behind us and God has decided to favor us with not only life sustained but life created.

The family tree has been decorated many times, but when Janet puts the little red cap on the top, something inside me stirs even now. I choke back a tear that only she might truly understand. That little cap is not just about our firstborn son but about the reminder that Christmas is about God doing the unexpected for the undeserving. He didn't give us a million dollars or send a star shooting through the sky. What happened to us happens millions of times every year around the world, and it was the simple gift that was the most significant. "Unto us a child is born." That sounds very familiar. It was the original Christmas message. It was a simple Christmas then, but on the Christmas of 1976, we understood just how precious and wonderful the gift of life truly was.

8.

Stability

So much had transpired between the Christmases of 1975 and 1976—first Janet's cancer and then the birth of our first child. But for the Christmas of 1977, we would have something very real to celebrate—the ownership of our first home.

My job with James Robison continued to bring increased responsibilities. His organization was growing rapidly through his television outreach as well as through large outdoor rallies and evangelistic meetings that he held in stadiums. My hours had been increased throughout the early part of 1977 even as I continued my classes at Southwestern and tried to be a good dad and husband. Janet and I had made the deliberate decision that she would be a full-time mother, and we determined that we would make the necessary sacrifices in our personal lives so John Mark would not have to spend more time with strangers than with us. We lived frugally but always believed that if we acted responsibly and walked by faith, our path would be clear. This is in no way intended to disparage parents who choose to keep their children in day care while both of them work or single parents who have no choice but to leave their children in the care of another. It's just that we knew it was right for us, though we recognized that it would mean setting very rigid financial priorities to make it work.

Despite a modest income, we never wavered in our commitment to tithe—to give a minimum of 10 percent of our gross income to our church. We did this not only because it was a doctrine of our faith but, more important, because it signified that everything we had was truly the Lord's, and we believed that the mere giving of a dime from each dollar was more than reasonable given what He had blessed us with. Plus, we had experienced the generosity of many people who had supported us in our time of need during Janet's illness, and we knew that one of the things we could do in return was to give to others as others had given to us.

I had started at the Robison organization doing radio spots and later started buying media and doing whatever else they needed me to do, which sometimes included menial tasks like emptying the trash or moving boxes. That was fine by me—I needed the hours and the type and the volume of work didn't matter. Throughout the spring of 1977, I balanced work and school and family as best I could. Robison had an in-house advertising agency that did everything from concept to completion in all sorts of advertising—from radio and TV to billboard creation and placement and print. We had graphic artists on staff (this was in the old days before computers, when artists worked with brushes, pencils, X-acto knives, and acetate overlays). We had people who wrote copy, produced ads, and packaged them. In addition to the obvious in-house work where we handled all advertising and marketing for James Robison, we did work for outside clients ranging from megachurches to parachurch organizations that worked alongside churches with their support and service.

I wrote copy, voiced radio and TV spots, placed all forms of ads for events in all media, and did research that James could use for articles, television, etc. In May of 1977, Gordon Waller, who had launched and directed Focus Advertising Agency, announced that he was leaving to go back to his native Alabama. Much to my surprise, James asked me if I was interested in taking the job of directing Focus Advertising and taking on the title of director of communications for the ministry. With this new job, I would travel with the crusade team to handle press announcements from the stage, and troubleshoot controversies that often arose from negative press during evangelistic meetings.

It was in so many ways the chance of a lifetime. I was just twenty-one years old, married with a not-yet-one-year-old child, and being asked to manage a staff of twelve people and a multimillion-dollar budget. I was the youngest person in the department, but I would oversee it. This was the job I had hoped to land since I was a teenager, but taking on a full-time job would mean leaving seminary.

One of my cherished professors at Southwestern was the late Dr. Oscar Thompson, a professor of evangelism. I asked to visit with him to seek his advice on whether to leave my studies and take this position or to spend the next year and a half completing my master's degree. I fully expected him to tell me that I needed to complete the degree first and not to let anything interrupt my studies.

I'll never forget the conversation. I told him what I had been offered but that it would be full time and would mean I would have to leave school. Dr. Thompson's response was surprising. He simply asked, "What did you come to seminary to train for?"

"A career in some type of Christian broadcasting," I replied.

"And what job are you being offered?" he asked, as if to say, "How plain does it have to get?" Then he smiled and waited for the obvious answer to sink in to me.

"I suppose if I've come to prepare for the very job I'm being offered, then maybe that's my answer," I managed to say.

His next piece of advice was classic Oscar Thompson profundity: "Mike, it looks to me as if the Lord is laying this in your lap. You have nothing to lose. It's the job that most people twice your age who already have their degree would die for. Go and do it. If it doesn't work out, I assure you that this seminary will still be sitting on this hill, but that job may not wait for you."

I never expected a seminary professor to advise me to leave school, but he affirmed for my head what my heart was already telling me.

I took the job and became director of communications for James Robison and the manager of Focus Advertising Agency. By today's standards, my pay would put me under the poverty line, but in 1977, the thirteen-thousand-dollar annual salary was more money than I had ever imagined being able to make.

The offices for James Robison were in Hurst, Texas, a suburb of Fort Worth in the Mid-Cities area located between Fort Worth and Dallas. Janet and I had been living near the seminary, at the southwestern part of Fort Worth. In traffic, it could be a forty-five minute drive or longer, and now, since there was no reason for us to live near the seminary campus, we decided it made sense to move closer to where I'd be working. We started looking.

James was willing to take a chance on me and believed that I was worth the risk of taking an untested and unknown twenty-one-year-old and handing him a huge level of responsibility. In the mid-seventies, James Robison's ministry was growing not only in size but also in controversy. He was as plainspoken and eloquent as anyone on the scene, and his bold and unfiltered form of preaching never left the crowd in doubt of where he stood on any given issue. Some reporters dubbed him God's angry prophet because of his calls for repentance and his denouncement of the sins he believed were destroying the nation.

It was unfortunate that many people knew him only from the headlines and didn't have the opportunity that I had to spend time with him one on one in planes, cars, and quiet settings without the public present. In his private life, he was an intense and focused, highly competitive, and very driven individual who genuinely believed that biblical messages should be presented with urgency, and he said he truly felt pain whenever he saw the anguish and anxiety of others. What made me appreciate him was that beneath that sometimes raw, earthy, and even brusque exterior was one of the kindest and most compassionate people I have ever known.

Immediately after I was hired, I was called to James's office by the executive director of the organization, Clayton Spriggs, who would later become like a father to me. I couldn't imagine what I might have done—good or bad—that would warrant an urgent meeting with James. As soon as I arrived in his office, James said, "I need you to come with me."

We drove to a nice men's clothing store in Hurst, and as we got out of the car, he said, "If you're going to work for me, I want you to look nice and represent me well. Let's get you some decent clothes."

I still wore the factory-outlet polyester knit suit that I had bought for $12.50, and I'm sure I must have looked like the ultimate country hick, but it was all I had. I was worried that it would take most of my new paycheck to pay for the kind of clothes in this store, which was more upscale than any store I ever had shopped in.

James must have sensed my terror at the thought of being obligated to purchase one or more suits and the accessories to go with it, so he told me, "I'm going to get you outfitted with everything you need to look sharp, and it will be my gift to you because I believe in you."

Normally, I would have immediately asked if there were any closeouts or out-of-season merchandise that was deeply discounted, but James took control and picked out three very nice suits and then personally selected shirts and ties to match. I would have been overwhelmed had he bought me one suit to replace my factory-outlet special, but I was completely stunned that he was apparently replacing my wardrobe.

Through the years, others may have said unkind things about James Robison, but not in my presence. Like all of us, he was a human being with some flaws, but his heart was as pure and authentic as that of anyone I've known. I will forever count him as a mentor and friend, one who believed in me for no outwardly apparent reason.

As Janet and her newly and nattily dressed husband looked for a place to live, one of the people at the office told us about a new development that was being built in the Mid-Cities area. The developer had purchased large areas of land and created entire neighborhoods with semicustom starter homes in which, even though the floor plan in each home was basically the same, the buyer was able to pick out several of the components, such as the exterior style, brick, roof, paint trim color, interior colors, carpet, and some fixtures. Because an entire street of houses were built at one time, large crews could be kept constantly busy with no downtime or travel time between houses. My friend from work and his wife were in the process of buying one, and he encouraged me to look into it for us.

The thought of our buying a home—and a new one at that—seemed absurd to a couple who struggled to make rent payments, let alone mortgage payments. We decided that it wouldn't hurt or cost us anything to go to the development and look at one of the model homes and at least confront the fact that we couldn't possibly purchase a house.

The houses were 1,200 to 1,300 square feet, with three bedrooms, two baths, an enclosed garage, a nice family room with a fireplace, a lawn, a kitchen with all the appliances, including a dishwasher and refrigerator, and central heat and air-conditioning. Each home was landscaped and the lawn seeded for grass as part of the package.

The Texas economy was on fire at that time, and this developer had found the perfect niche market of mostly young, first-time home buyers. For a mere hundred-dollar deposit, a purchaser could hold one of the houses, apply for a loan that their own finance company would finance, and choose their floor plan, colors, and details.

We laugh about it now, but the $100 was a big deal to us then. What if we didn't get approved and lost our $100? That would be a real setback for us. The total purchase price was $28,500 and the payments would be $288 per month. That wasn't too much more than we'd have to pay in rent for anything decent in the Mid-Cities area, and we'd be doing something at age twenty-one that my parents hadn't been able to do until I was in high school—own the house we lived in. Janet was almost shaking as she wrote the check for the $100 and we made a deposit on a house. The difference between buying a home and renting one was like the difference between putting something in concrete and putting it in sand. It meant that we would be putting down roots and weren't just a couple of crazy kids getting married, but adults who were embarking upon the ultimate symbol of the American dream—owning a home.

We were able to watch as our house was built from the slab up. Neither of us had ever lived in a house that was brand new. It was a long way from the little duplex in Arkadelphia that we had rented just two years earlier for forty dollars a month.

The house was to be ready in early to mid-December, and we could move in then. We applied for the loan and were approved without any problems. Janet's mother gave us new bedroom furniture for Christmas that year, and we used the furniture we had had in our last home for one of the other bedrooms. We would have our master bedroom, John Mark would have a room, and we'd even have a spare guest room for when relatives or friends came. My dad drove to Fort Worth in his pickup truck and rented a U-Haul trailer so we could move what possessions we had to our new home. There is one advantage to not having much—it's much easier to move—and we quickly got everything moved into 7445 Tunbridge Drive in North Richland Hills, Texas, the address of our very first house.

Just in time for Christmas, we had something truly spectacular to celebrate. We were homeowners. We didn't have to ask a landlord if it was okay to trim hedges or put a nail in the wall to hang a picture. We didn't have to worry if the rent would unexpectedly go up when we were least prepared for it. We didn't have to argue over who was responsible for paying to fix a broken toilet or unclog a drain. True, now *we* had to pay for all of this routine maintenance, but we would be paying for it in *our* house, not someone else's. In short, instead of being controlled, we had control, and it felt great. Very grown up and stable.

Our first Christmas in our new house was as special as any we'd had. We threw a Christmas party and invited friends who oohed and aahed that we had such a fresh, new place to dwell. They knew where we had lived before, with chipping paint, splintery wood floors, old fixtures and appliances, and tiny rooms that were drafty cold in the winter unless you stood right by the gas space heater and miserably hot in the summer unless you sat directly in front of the window air conditioner or one of the little electric fans we used to blow air from room to room.

The house on Tunbridge really wasn't that great by most people's standards today. It was structurally sound but obviously wasn't built with Italian marble or handcrafted woodwork, nor was it adorned with authentic Persian rugs or expensive works of art. But to us, it was a little slice of heaven for a young couple who had lived in some places that could best be described as little slices of hell.

Plus, it was great to be able to give John Mark a place to live where we didn't have to worry that the cockroaches were bigger than he was. We truly loved that little house, and to us at the time, it was huge.

In time for Christmas, Janet decorated the brick hearth around the fireplace and hung John Mark's Christmas stocking on the mantle. She found just the Christmas tree she wanted, and my parents gave us some lights and a few ornaments that were surplus from their own collection. And of course, at the top of our tree, we placed the little red cap that a year earlier had sat on John Mark's red head. The hat didn't fit his head anymore, but it fit just perfectly on the top of that tree.

While we always looked forward to going home to Arkansas for Christmas to be with our families, that was one year when it was really hard to pack the car and drive away from a place that we were so grateful to live in. And so grateful to *own*. We had a house. *Our* house. Most people will probably think it strange that we were so thrilled just to have a house, and we admit, it was a pretty simple house. But we were getting really used to being happy with simple things. And this house made Christmas really special—a special but simple Christmas!

9.

Limitations

As much as I love Christmas, it almost caused me to convert to Judaism. The religious part of the holiday is fine with me, so don't gasp and think I was ready to abandon my faith. The problem with Christmas had nothing to do with Jesus. In fact, that *was* the problem—Christmas wasn't about Jesus anymore. And it was this fact that had me wondering if maybe it was time to find another way altogether to observe the holiday.

One of the big differences between a Christmas in poverty and one in prosperity is that prosperity creates some real serious complications and complexities. The more material things we have, the more likely we are to be really stressed around Christmas, especially if we have kids. Granted, given the choice between prosperity and poverty, I would choose prosperity every time, but it's hard to have a simple Christmas when you have to worry not only about getting the right gift for your kid but also that you get him enough to keep him busy for a while.

Being a father is the greatest joy I've ever known, but it's also the scariest job I've ever had and by far the most challenging. Governing a state is a piece of cake compared to being a dad, and that's why, whenever a reporter asks me, "What do you regard as your most significant accomplishment?" I always answer the same way: "Being a dad."

I'm sure this answer surprises some reporters, who expect me to extol the impact of education reform in my state, or the health initiatives that brought national attention to Arkansas, or the rebuilding of our highways, or even running for president or writing books that have made it to the *New York Times* bestseller list. None of that. Raising three kids who turned out okay—that's the big deal. It was far tougher than all the other stuff.

Part of what makes fatherhood so difficult is Christmas. This is especially true when the little tykes are small and Dad is expected to perform the "manly" function of putting their toys together. And that's what almost drove me to Judaism.

I've always been mechanically challenged, and I realized it at an early age, when my jack-of-all-trades dad tried to teach me the rudiments of being a do-it-yourselfer.

Dorsey Huckabee was one of those people who could fix toilets or faucets, wire an appliance or light fixture, fix a car, build a room onto a house, or even build a go-cart from scratch. Now, sometimes his products were hardly "factory-looking," but they worked. Thank goodness, because had some of his attempts failed, my sister and I would have had the double embarrassment of having something that not only looked like crap but also didn't work.

My dad was a utilitarian—not an artist. His stuff worked, but he never would have won design awards and people didn't gush over the aesthetic "wow" factor of the stuff he made. For him, fixing or making things was about saving a buck, and we must have saved a bunch of them, because anything someone else offered to do professionally my father figured he could do on his own for free.

Even though he built or repaired a lot of stuff, he didn't have to deal with the ominous challenge of Christmas as much as I did. For one thing, the fact that we didn't have the money to afford a room full of gifts meant that there wasn't that much to put together in the first place, and in the fifties and sixties, most stuff came pretty much put together and required little assembly anyway. All a kid had to do was open the box and start playing with whatever was inside. Easy for the kid and a relief for the parents. Sometimes batteries had to be inserted, but even a kid could do that. Of course, it was always a real downer when the box said "batteries not included" and your parents had forgotten to get batteries and you had to sit there on Christmas morning with a dumb look on your face wondering what the toy would do or sound like until the day after Christmas when the stores were open and you could finally get batteries.

Even though my dad didn't have to put many toys together, he was still remarkably more adept and productive with his hands than his only son, who would generally just throw a part across the room if it didn't fit where it was supposed to.

One Christmas I wanted a go-cart. They were popular with

kids, and I knew better than to ask for a '57 Chevy, so I figured this was the next best thing. At the age of seven, I didn't have any idea how much a go-cart might cost, nor did I care. It was my job to want things. It was my parents' responsibility to figure out how to get them. A gasoline-powered go-cart was just what I wanted.

There was no way my dad was going to spend a month's pay on a go-cart. Heck, he could make one! And that's just what he did. He took an engine from an old lawn mower, welded a frame from scrap metal he got from the junkyard, found some little tires that probably had once belonged to a lawn tractor, and somehow cobbled together a go-cart. He was proud, and rightly so, of his creation and even more proud that he had managed to save enough money to impress a Saudi prince. I'm sure when I saw it, my face didn't convey the level of gratitude that I should have expressed. I was, of course, hoping for one that looked like the ones in the Sears catalog, and this one didn't. Think Jed Clampett's truck on *The Beverly Hillbillies* compared to a Corvette, and you get the picture of how my dad's homemade go-cart compared to the one I had imaged in my mind over and over.

To his credit, the old man did build a functioning machine, and after I got over the initial shock of its crude appearance and the fact that its engine had once mowed the lawn of some nice family on the other side of town, I did have fun riding it around the neighborhood.

Maybe my father's sometimes rather less than superb flair for design was tempered by his desire to give his kids all he could with the resources he had. One thing is for sure—he was not one to go into debt for things he couldn't afford. It was his Depression-era mind-set that caused him to think this way. He believed that the bottom could fall out at any moment and we should prepare for the worst because it was probably going to happen. My dad was also one of those guys who believed that if such a calamity were to strike and it only affected one family, it would probably be ours. So we always lived as if an apocalypse was about to strike our house, storing massive amounts of toilet paper and paper towels just in case. We might be turned into dust particles by a nuclear blast, but by gosh, there would be plenty of paper towels to wipe up the mess!

I know that my lack of proficiency with tools was a big disappointment to my dad. I think by the time I was lieutenant governor of Arkansas, he had finally made peace with the fact that I couldn't change the oil in my car without making a complete mess and that my one attempt to unclog a stopped drain resulted in a plumber having to be called to my house for an emergency visit to repair my "repair" and stop the resulting water that was gushing in our kitchen. My efforts to avoid the cost of the plumber resulted in a $1,200 plumbing bill, a huge mess in the kitchen, and a wife who could have frozen the Gobi Desert with her stare. My father died just three months before I was sworn in as governor, and I really wished he could have lived long enough to see that, just so he might finally feel I had redeemed myself. He probably would have said at the swearing in, "Son, I'm proud you made governor, but I sure wish you could use a table saw."

Power tools and me? Not a good combination. It's like trying to get Dick Cheney and Osama bin Laden together to watch football and eat pizza. Never going to happen. I'm certain that part of my clumsiness with all things mechanical comes from the fact that I should have been left-handed, but my mother thought left-handedness would make it hard for me to be "normal" in a right-handed world, so she always put the pencil or crayon in my right hand and through her stern discipline and perseverance taught me to live right-handedly. At least somewhat. I bat, shoot a rifle or shotgun, and play putt-putt golf left-handed. I write, shoot a pistol, and eat with my right hand. When people ask if I'm left- or right-handed, I usually just say that I'm ambidextrous. When I broke a finger on my right hand playing Little League baseball as a child, I was forced to eat and write left-handed while my hand was in a cast. I was able to do both rather easily, and now I'm able to use a fork in either hand and my writing is equally illegible regardless of which hand I've used. In fact, my handwriting is so bad that I can't even read it myself and try to avoid writing as much as possible unless I need to sign something. My personal assistant during my tenure both as lieutenant governor and as governor, Dawn Cook, is the only human I know who can decode my penmanship. I would actually ask her to read things I had written to tell me what they said because I couldn't make them out.

For much of my childhood and adolescence, I felt guilty over my inability to work with simple tools, so I married someone who is pretty good at it. Janet is the "handywoman" in our house and has repaired our washer (put new timers and gears in it) and dryer (changed the heating element and timer) and done minor repairs around the house. She has also helped build houses in over forty states and many foreign countries through her work with Habitat for Humanity. Because she is so active with Habitat and has served on its international board for a number of years, people assume that I volunteer with her on the construction projects. Whenever anyone asks me about this, I always say the same thing—I would never spend the night in a house that I helped build!

So now that you understand just how "dexterity challenged" I am, you can better understand why, for me, what should be a heavenly holiday—Christmas—became the holiday from hell.

By the time John Mark was born, the days of buying toys that didn't require any assembly were as gone as the days of 78 rpm records. From my earliest "dad days," I couldn't actually purchase an item, but rather ended up with a box of parts and an instruction manual that had been written in Japanese or Mandarin and poorly translated into broken English so that a mechanical engineer would have had a difficult time understanding it. The notion that "Mr. Thumbs" (aka me) would be able to put even supposedly simple things together was laughable, but my pride and ego compelled me to try.

The idea of selling things to consumers that have to be completely constructed from scratch was an evolutionary thing. It started with things coming ready to take out of the box and use, then progressed to "batteries not included," and then came the innocent enough label "some assembly required," meaning that the package contained two or three large pieces that would easily fit together and the product required nothing more than simple observation to make it work. I wasn't fortunate enough to do my "daddying" during those golden days of American toydom. By the time it fell upon me to prepare the Christmas toys for the big day, the assembly of almost anything other than a stuffed animal required a minimum of a master's degree in mechanical engineering from MIT and four or five assistants who had previously helped assemble space shuttles for NASA. I'm sure it won't be long before the stuffed animals will come packaged as a bag of stuffing, some cloth material, plastic pieces for eyes, nose, and accessories, and a little sewing kit so the consumer can build the teddy bear from the pieces and parts.

Right after John Mark's third birthday in 1979, we were in the process of moving from Texas back to Arkansas and Janet and I thought it was time for him to get his first tricycle. This is always a milestone in a child's life—the day he extends movement beyond his own legs and employs a mechanical device to move him more efficiently and quickly. I had loved my tricycle when I was a kid and pretty much worn it out riding up and down the sidewalks of my neighborhood and around my house on rainy days. I was sure that no child could turn out normal without a bike, so I was excited to buy John Mark's first "vehicle" and teach him how to ride.

I attempted to purchase an already-assembled tricycle from each of the local stores that sold them and was virtually laughed out of the store for daring to request such a thing. "Those are floor display models," I was brutally told, and my attempt to buy one was met with derision. Logic was no weapon in this endeavor. I pointed out that the floor models were likely shipped to the store as a box full of parts and that whoever put them together had obviously done a good job, so why not sell me one and let that experienced tricycle engineer simply put another together? No can do, they told me. I offered to pay to have their guy do it (a practice I must have inspired, since now I see that service offered regularly by stores) but was rebuffed.

My son was going to have a tricycle no matter what! Of course, the smart thing would have been to buy the box of bolts and metal pieces and ask my dad (the grandpa) or even my wife to assemble it. But having to admit that I was a total wimp who couldn't even assemble a tricycle would have been emasculating to me. I mean, it was a tricycle, not an ultralight airplane or a rocket ship. How hard could it be? So armed with my manly pride and all the confidence I could muster, I purchased a tricycle at Wal-Mart, took the box home, and announced to Janet that I would put it together on Christmas Eve after John Mark went to bed. Janet offered to help, but of course I waved off any assistance, as that would have directly threatened my manhood and I might as well start carrying a purse.

It's a little tricycle, for heaven's sake! I should have known better and simply let Janet put it together, but no—I was out to prove that being a dad had magically endowed me with new powers to do for my son at Christmas what every other American dad did for his son.

Once we put John Mark to bed around eight thirty on Christmas Eve, I immediately went to the garage, which would be the staging area for this momentous event. The tricycle was no longer a toy for my boy—it was the symbol of my manhood and ability to celebrate Christmas the way God intended.

As I opened the box, I was a bit intimidated by the fact that there were what seemed like about four hundred little plastic packets, each of which had a different size screw, nut, and washer, along with dozens of larger parts that, when put together, were supposed to form a tricycle. No two pieces had been attached or assembled in any way. I'm sure that various pieces of the little three-wheeled challenge had been fabricated in various manufacturing plants around the world, and now I had before me a collection of parts and a very pathetic excuse for a parts list and instruction manual that contained indecipherable instructions and a few pencil sketches to illustrate what the end result should look like.

The first challenge was simply trying to figure out which size screw was what and how they fit into the overall picture. They all looked alike to me, and the variations in size weren't distinguishable based on the pictures in the manual.

I would have been better able to figure out the Rubik's Cube while blindfolded. Concern began to give way to sheer panic— my son would wake up on Christmas morning and I would present him with a floor filled with various pieces of bright red tubular metal, some little wheels, and several large piles of hardware. I would announce, "Merry Christmas, son! Santa brought you a tricycle!"

I could imagine him looking at the entire floor covered with unconnected pieces and bursting into tears thinking that Santa's elves must have unionized and gone on strike. Then I would have to listen to his mother chide me for having ruined Christmas, not just for John Mark but for the entire planet. Somehow, I was sure she would blame me for ruining the spirit of the holiday through my laziness and pride.

I couldn't let this get to me! I labored on, attempting to find pieces of the puzzle that either would fit or could be forced to connect with one another.

The project that should have taken about an hour was consuming the entire night. Janet checked on me to ask how it was going, and of course, I lied like a snake and told her it was going just fine. She went to bed around midnight and I again lied and said I should be headed that way soon. That part wasn't as bad a lie—it was true that I *should* be headed that way, but what should be and what was were totally different things.

By four o'clock on Christmas morning, something remotely resembling a tricycle sat in the middle of the garage. And you know what? It turns out I didn't need all those screws, nuts, and washers after all, because I had a pile of them left over that I hadn't been able to fit.

I placed the trike under the tree just in time for John Mark to wake up and go into the family room, where the tree proudly stood with his little Christmas hat from his first Christmas topping it. There was that red, shiny tricycle in all its glory— well, most of its glory, since there were some parts missing.

For reasons that I still do not fully understand, that little tricycle always squeaked, and no amount of WD-40 could make it stop. I assured John Mark that it was just the equivalent of motor noise and that it would help us locate him if he was riding about the neighborhood.

Another thing that was a bit odd about the tricycle was that with each revolution of the back left wheel, the entire bike leaned slightly to the left. It was as if it were limping on a sore tire. Despite all of my creative communication skills, I couldn't find a way to euphemistically explain to John Mark why his tricycle had this very distinct disability. He seemed to accept that limitation, although I don't think his mother ever forgave me for having refused her assistance in building it in the first place. And I have wished for the past thirty years that I had asked for her help. In fact, what I probably should have done is said, "This tricycle assembly looks really easy and shouldn't take but a few minutes. I think I'll just let you go ahead and put it together and I'll get our Christmas music lined up on the cassette player for Christmas morning."

I learned a lot from my dismal failure at seeking to be the "big-shot dad" by attempting to put that little tricycle together by myself. As Clint Eastwood said in *Magnum Force*, "A man's got to know his limitations."

I learned some of mine on that long Christmas Eve night. Knowing our limitations and not trying to do things outside our capacity often means we have to break down our pride and admit we need help. I don't buy things that require assembly unless there is someone (wife, son, etc.) who has agreed in advance to put them together. I don't need to waste money on an item I can't figure out, and I don't have the time to go through the endless frustration of my utter ineptness at all things requiring manual dexterity.

I have come to learn that Christmas is about accepting more than just my limitations in the assembly of toys and appliances. It's about accepting that I'm incapable of putting my own life together and making all the pieces fit. It's about recognizing that God isn't asking me to impress Him with my skills at "building a perfect human being." He didn't send His son to criticize my failures or laugh at my very miserable attempts at putting all the screws, nuts, and washers in my life in the right place. In fact, His son became a carpenter so he'd really have the hang of patiently building something from the rawest of materials.

There's nothing disgraceful about admitting the need for help. The real disgrace is being so filled with pride and ego that we don't reach out for the help that we so obviously need, and in the end we fail anyway.

My limitations in toy building may have almost made me convert to Judaism, but they also showed me that this is what Christmas is all about. We are not alone. God has already reached out to us before we even ask for Him. He can handle my limitations, and so should I.

Once I fully realized this, I understood that Christmas wasn't the problem. It was the answer. I was the problem. But I could fix this by finally accepting my limitations and remembering Christmas for what it really is. Simple. Powerful and profound, but simple.

10.

Transitions

Christmas is, in many ways, a milestone that marks various parts of our year. We will put things off "until after Christmas" or commit to get something done "before Christmas." We speak of Christmas as a reference point in time, as in "We haven't seen them since last Christmas." For many of us Christmas is the biggest and most anticipated holiday of the year, and it's thought of not just as a day but as an entire season. Christmas is also the time when you catch up with many people in your life—family, friends, neighbors—whom you might not have spoken to in a while. It's a time to reflect on life—what you're doing, what you've done, and what you hope to do.

It's also a time of transition—from one year to the next—so it shouldn't come as too big a surprise that some of the most significant transitions and turning points in my life have occurred around Christmas. Janet and I left Arkansas to move to Texas after her bout with spinal cancer right at Christmas, and we moved into our first house just a few weeks before Christmas. But since then we've experienced several more Christmas transitions that have greatly affected the course of our lives as a whole.

From the time I was in elementary school, I read the daily newspaper, watched TV news, and listened to news on the radio. I kept up with current events and the news of the day more than most adults I knew and certainly more than most of the kids my age. Politics and current events captivated me, and even though I couldn't for the life of me see how I would do it, I couldn't help but think that one day I would run for office. At one time, I thought about becoming a lawyer, but after landing a job at the local radio station when I was a teenager, I realized that the best way I could serve God was to work in broadcasting. I liked the work and was good at it, and I figured it might also be a good way to eventually launch a career in politics. At various times in my life, I would think about running for office, and then circumstances, such as my becoming a pastor, would kill that vision and render it seemingly impossible. Contrary to popular belief, my decision to move back to Arkansas was not so I could become a minister; I wanted to run for office.

For all the talk about how dumb politicians are and how they tend to follow instead of lead, the greatest examples of sheep following sheep are those in the media who will hear or read something from one of their colleagues and, without any attempt to find out if it's true, report it as fact.

If you followed the coverage of the 2008 Republican presidential primary, you would probably assume I was preaching in a little Baptist church in Arkansas until one glorious Sunday I up and decided to run for president. A pretty dramatic story, but a bogus one nonetheless. The true story wouldn't have been that hard to have discovered, and even when a few reporters asked me about it directly, they ignored the facts in order to maintain the image of me as a one-dimensional "religious" candidate who had no experience leading outside the church and no motive for going into politics except to advance my agenda. They ignored the fact that I had more executive experience actually running a government than any of the candidates in the race from either party except for Tommy Thompson, the former governor of Wisconsin, who left the race in August of 2007. Journalists barely mentioned my time as governor or the initiatives I had achieved in such areas as education, health care, the prison system, environment, taxes, and the economy, which had attracted national accolades.

What most people don't realize, thanks in large part to this one-sided coverage of my career, was that my decision to become a pastor was actually a detour from what I thought I would be doing. My career goal was in communications—radio, television, advertising, and writing, primarily with Christian organizations and ministries. And this is what I was doing in September 1980 when the congregation of the Immanuel Baptist Church in Pine Bluff, Arkansas, invited me to speak in their pastorless church one Sunday and then asked me to serve as their interim pastor while they searched for someone to fill the post full time. I had recently created my own Christian communications company, Mike Huckabee and Associates, and so was able to work at the church and at my day job for a while. Janet and I had in fact made an offer on a home back in Hope and expected to move back there, since there was really no reason for us to stay in Texas anymore. It would also give me the opportunity to reestablish my residency in Arkansas, since I was starting to consider running for Congress in the Fourth Congressional District, which mostly comprises southern Arkansas.

I had thought that President Jimmy Carter was going to usher in a new kind of politics and lead the nation past what had been a tumultuous period—Watergate. But less than a year into his presidency, I realized that his policies were warmed-over classic big-government liberalism, and I grew increasingly restless about the direction of the nation. I had hoped that Ronald Reagan would win the GOP nomination in 1976, and in 1980 when he announced his decision to run for the White House, I was truly encouraged. My own political views had grown more conservative over the years, bolstered by cassette tapes of speeches by Paul Weyrich and Howard Phillips and books by people like Phyllis Schlafly. I sensed that the country was disenchanted with the liberalism of the Democratic Party and that 1980 would be a watershed year for conservatives. I was barely old enough to run for Congress, but it seemed like the right time to start preparing for what I thought was going to be my first political race. I talked to some key leaders in the state GOP and even had conversations with some of the leading old-school Democratic leaders, just to get their take on the political landscape.

I was enjoying being an interim pastor but expected that to

be a short-term gig that would end in a few months when the church secured a permanent pastor. But to my surprise, after nearly three months as the interim pastor at Immanuel, the church asked me if I wanted to take on the job permanently. After much prayer and consideration, Janet and I agreed to make the move to Pine Bluff permanent. We forfeited the deposit on our house in Hope, I shut down my small business and notified my clients that I would not be able to provide them services after the first of the year, and at the age of twenty-five, I became the pastor of some of the most wonderful people in the world. Because I had more experience in communications and advertising than in preaching, I had a steep learning curve and approached the job with a very nontraditional style. The pulpit duties were a point of comfort for me, but working with deacons, committees, and special-interest groups was all new. I will say that nothing better prepared me for a future political career quite like experiencing the politics of a local Baptist church!

In addition to my role as pastor, I helped the church develop a logo and a "branded strategy" for advertising, purchase ad space on bus benches, and launch a daily radio commentary on the local news/talk station called "Positive Alternatives." The station, KOTN, was overwhelmingly the dominant station in that market, and at first the manager was very reluctant to sell airtime to a local church for the two-minute-a-day (morning and afternoon) drive-time spots that I wanted to do. I told him I was going to do a motivational and inspirational commentary that would appeal to everyone and promised that it wouldn't be "in your face" religious broadcasting. He agreed to take it on a trial basis, and it became one of the station's most popular features. The station manager, Buddy Deane, even became a dear friend of mine over the years despite his original doubts about putting a Baptist program on his station. In fact, when Buddy died years later, during my time as governor, I was asked to conduct his funeral service.

Our church was very innovative in terms of its communications and also launched a twenty-four-hour-a-day television channel that broadcast not only church services but also talk shows, sports, and local events. Looking back, I am amazed that we had the chutzpah to attempt something so bold, but it worked, and the church grew dramatically and rapidly because of it.

I settled in to the role of pastor and loved it. I abandoned the idea of ever running for office, assuming that being a pastor would preclude me from ever being able to make that transition to politics. During my six years in Pine Bluff, we added two more children to our growing family—David, who was born just a few months prior to our moving there, and Sarah, born in 1982. It was also there that I learned not only some useful skills in everything from diplomacy to administration but also some of the most important lessons of my life.

A pastor looks at life more deeply than people in most other professions. A pastor witnesses the most wonderful moments in a person's life, such as weddings and births, as well as the most painful moments, such as divorce, disease, and death. During my time as a pastor, I received an education like no other in the realities of life. I saw intense poverty by going into the homes of the poorest people in our community to bring food or assist in a family crisis, and I saw intense prosperity by interacting with some of the most successful businesspeople in the community.

Most elected officials learn about the issues of the day by studying or reading about them. For me, there is not a single social pathology that I haven't seen firsthand, and I probably have a story for any situation you could think of: a pregnant unwed teen afraid to tell her parents that she's about to be a mother; a young couple faced with the news that their child will be born with severe disabilities; a middle-aged couple forced to become "parents" to their parents, who are no longer able to care for themselves; an elderly couple having to decide whether to take medicine or eat because they can't afford to do both. I've met couples facing marital or financial problems; individuals with drug, alcohol, gambling, sex, or other addictions; and people suffering from deep depression. I saw all of this every week and spent a good bit of my time counseling those who had come to me as their first line of help for just about anything and everything.

After six years in Pine Bluff, I was approached by the pastor search committee of the Beech Street First Baptist Church in Texarkana, Arkansas. Other pastor search committees had approached me in the past, but I had always declined their offers. But the Texarkana congregation was persistent, and in order to test their seriousness, I told them that I would only consider working at their church if they were willing to launch a television channel similar to what we had in Pine Bluff. I believed that part of my calling was to use the media as a communication vessel for the Gospel, and so I wasn't willing to give up the opportunity to do that, no matter where I worked. Because the Beech Street First Baptist Church was known as a more traditional church, I fully expected this to be a deal breaker for them, but they told me that it was precisely this nontraditional approach and the idea of a television channel that appealed to them and had led them to me.

Several weeks of discussion and agonizing prayer followed. Janet, the kids, and I loved Pine Bluff and the people who lived there. I could have stayed there forever. We were very active in the community, we had close friends, and the kids were settled in school and the neighborhood. But despite how comfortable we were, we somehow knew that, despite our misgivings, we were being clearly drawn to a new field of ministry and life and that God was calling us to a new chapter of our lives. We decided to move to Texarkana.

Our experience in Texarkana was very different from our experience in Pine Bluff, but equally exciting and fulfilling. I hit the ground running by launching a major fund-raising effort to start the television channel, construct a family life center that had been on the drawing board for years but never constructed, and purchase additional property for the church to expand. The church was a majestic old building originally constructed in the early 1900s and was rich with history and tradition. It was a landmark in the city for its distinctive silver dome, which made it look more like a state capitol than a church. Because it was an older, downtown church, it was much more traditional than I what was used to, and one of the regular challenges I faced was taking my more unconventional methods of ministry into a much more conventional congregation.

I immersed myself in the community just as I had in Pine Bluff, and Janet and I found a wonderful home on a cul-de-sac in an absolutely great neighborhood. There were kids everywhere who were about the same age as ours, and it was a quiet, safe, and uncongested area about as perfect as we could have hoped for. We loved our house, and with its five bedrooms and spacious yard, we had room for the kids to play and to enjoy life.

Over the next six years, we lived a life that was nothing short of ideal. We were in a wonderful church and had close friends with whom we developed deep bonds. My sister, Pat, already lived in Texarkana at that time, and my parents and in-laws were just thirty miles away in Hope, so we saw our families more than we ever had. My parents moved to Texarkana about two years later and lived just a few blocks from my sister and from us.

Neither Janet nor I had grown up with all that much, and while we were far from rich and still had to live frugally, we were enjoying a standard of living far better than either of us had growing up. We were active in the community, our kids were totally engaged in all sorts of sports and school activities, and we truly loved the life we were living—neighborhood, community, church, family. We had lots of friends, and I really can't think of any enemies. Great fishing lakes were nearby, and we were only a three-hour drive from Arlington Stadium, home of the Texas Rangers baseball team, whom we would go to see play several times each year. Life was good!

In 1989, I was elected president of the Arkansas Baptist State Convention and became the youngest person to ever hold that position. I was thirty-four years old. It was a tumultuous time in the life of Southern Baptists, mainly due to a decade-long struggle over the doctrinal direction of the denomination. The theological issues had been overwhelmingly settled in the favor of an unapologetic commitment to the authority and in-errancy of the Bible, and about the only thing left to fight about was not what belief system to follow, but who would hold key positions in the church. My election was viewed as a way to put in office someone who was an unwavering conservative but who had not been divisive and was very involved in advancing the mission of the denomination. The other person nominated was Ronnie Floyd, a good friend of mine, who today is one of our nation's most dynamic and innovative pastors in Spring-dale and Rogers, Arkansas, and leads one of the most influen-tial ministries in the denomination. I've often joked with him that he may have gotten the better end of the deal by *not* being elected!

During my tenure, the denomination was able to avoid the angry schisms that had befallen other state conventions, and we had a peaceful and productive two years. To be fair, this had far less to do with me than it did with the rank-and-file pastors in Arkansas who kept the "main thing the *main thing*." The main thing in this case was the goal of equipping people with biblical truth so they could live out the Gospel and mimic the life of Christ in their everyday lives. Being elected president of the state convention put me in a highly visible position not only with Arkansas Baptists but in other states as well. Southern Baptists make up 20 percent of the population of Arkansas, making it by far the largest denomination in the state. I received very favorable news coverage during my time as president, from both secular and denominational publications, and I traveled all over the state as a representative of the convention.

By early 1991, several good friends and others had asked me, "Have you ever thought about running for office?" While most of them had no idea of my plans some eleven years earlier to do just that, some of my old friends from high school and college, to whom I had mentioned those plans twenty years earlier, also encouraged me to consider it.

In early spring of 1991, the Arkansas legislature was considering some prolife legislation that then-Governor Bill Clinton's Health Department director, Dr. Joycelyn Elders (later appointed surgeon general under President Bill Clinton) was openly opposing. At one legislative hearing, Dr. Elders made the now-infamous statement that "preachers need to get over their love affair with a fetus" and that "preachers need to quit moralizing from the pulpit."

The outrage was instant and intense. It was a direct insult to the character and integrity not only of pastors but of all prolife people in the state. Arkansas had passed an amendment to the state constitution in 1988 that declared a person to exist from the point of conception, and the state had a responsibility to protect human life until its natural conclusion. Not only were the pastors of the state incensed, but so were the voters, and a firestorm erupted throughout the state.

On several occasions during my tenure as Baptist Convention president, Governor Clinton contacted me to ask for input from the evangelical community. He was a shrewd and savvy politician and knew that the combined influence of Southern

Baptists alone could turn an issue. While the debate over abortion raged, Governor Clinton called and asked if I would be willing to sit down privately with Dr. Elders and explain how evangelicals felt about the issue and why there was such a strong, visceral reaction to her comments. I agreed, and the governor's staff set up the meeting between Dr. Elders and me at her office.

She and I met for almost two hours. It was a thoughtful and civil conversation, and to this day, we've maintained a cordial relationship, but our views on the sanctity of life and the role of government in such issues were 180 degrees apart. When I arrived home that night after the two-and-a-half hour drive from Little Rock to Texarkana, I told Janet, "If these are the people who are setting the agenda for our children's future in school and in the community, then maybe we're going to have to get out of the stands and onto the field." At the time I said that, I had no idea what it would lead to, but I knew that sitting back and letting others decide this issue wasn't enough.

Over the coming months, more people talked to me about the idea of running for office, and I began to seek counsel from trusted friends and other pastors. In several cases, I sought the advice of those who I thought for sure would discourage me, but to my surprise, I received encouragement. One of my mentors was Dr. Trueman Moore, a pastor in Fort Smith, Arkansas, and one of the most brilliant and thoughtful men I have ever known. He had become a source of inspiration and information for me, and I cherished his insights and respected his irreproachable integrity. I specifically sought him out assuming that he would discourage any notions I had about running for office. I was surprised when he said, "I would ordinarily advise a pastor to do what you're already doing, but in your case, I really feel that you should consider politics—we need people like you."

One of my close friends since the days we had met at Arkansas Boys State in 1972 was Jonathan Barnett of Siloam Springs, Arkansas. (Boys State is a national program operated in each state by the American Legion to build citizenship and patriotism in young men.) I had been elected governor of Boys State, and he had been elected as one of the two national Boys State senators from Arkansas. In high school, we had talked about one day going into politics, and he had become a leader in state and local Republican circles, chairing the county organization of Benton County, the largest and most influential county. As I visited with him to get his insights, he suggested I get to know some other political operatives and activists and told me some people I should contact.

As the fall of 1991 began to turn toward winter, Janet and I had seriously contemplated the idea of my running for the United States Senate and determined that it would be absurd for me to even entertain the notion. Bill Clinton had announced his candidacy for president in October of 1991, and we knew that that alone would change the political landscape of the state.

We carefully sought to weigh all the ramifications of stepping out from what was a very comfortable and desirable life to get into something that would be an incredibly uphill climb. To get elected, I would have to defeat Dale Bumpers, a three-term U.S. senator and two-term governor. As Christmas approached, we knew that to run in 1992 I would have to make my decision soon and that if I decided to run, it would require another major transition in our lives that would bring upheaval to the peaceful and comfortable world we lived in.

In December of 1991, within days of Christmas, Janet and I took a long walk around the streets of our neighborhood and talked very honestly with each other about what might be the most game-changing decision of our marriage and our lives. It was a cool but not especially cold night, and we were able to take our time as we walked past the nicely decorated homes in our well-groomed subdivision, where our friends and neighbors were behind their doors preparing for Christmas, oblivious to the fact that just outside, Janet and I were on a journey that wouldn't just end when we got back home. In fact, what happened on that walk would ultimately lead us further from home than we could have ever imagined.

Christmas is the perfect time to reflect; it's a time for looking back. You look back to the first Christmas, to the year behind you, and to the year ahead. At Christmas, you are reminded what really matters—sacrifice, love, family, purpose—and this Christmas was no different. Janet and I were grateful for everything we had, but we also knew that politics would give me the opportunity to give back even more. First, we knew that running for office would mean having to resign from the church, and that meant walking away from a good income and a comfortable life—better than either of us had imagined living. It would mean opening our lives up to a level of scrutiny, hostility, and criticism unlike any we had faced. We couldn't fully understand just how lonely the journey would be at times and how much it would empty us of pretty much everything we had materially, personally, and spiritually. But we decided that we could hardly encourage people to be "salt and light" in a broken world if we weren't willing to step out of the boat and into the sea ourselves.

Somewhere along Cambridge Street, where our house sat at the end of the cul-de-sac, Janet and I decided that if God's purpose and plan for our lives was to get comfortable, then we had indeed found success. But how could we truly claim that God's purpose for us was to become comfortable? We agreed that we were on the planet to be light in the darkness and a preservative in a culture that was spoiling.

It was our custom to have a Christmas open house for our church family each holiday season, and that year, as we welcomed the several hundred people—many of them dear friends—who dropped in throughout the day, it was difficult to hold back the deep emotions that were going through our minds. I must confess that the thought of leaving such a gracious circle of affirmation was painful. I would later compare the move from the church to politics to stepping out of a nice, warm, soothing hot tub and into a tank of hungry sharks!

As we celebrated the Christmas of 1991, we were aware that no matter what, things would never be the same in our lives. We had no idea of just how different they would be for the next eighteen years. We waited until after Christmas to tell the kids about the decision, though they could tell that something major was in the air. We wanted to keep things as normal as possible for as long as possible, and I'm glad we did, because from that Christmas forward, there would be nothing normal whatsoever about our lives.

On the last Sunday of 1991, I announced my intention to step down as pastor of the church effective the first week of February. I wanted to make sure there was an opportunity to tie up loose ends and make the transition as smooth as possible for the church, the staff, and the family. I did not say what had led me to this decision, as I didn't want anyone to think I was using the pulpit to advance my bid for office.

It was one of the most frightening risks Janet and I had taken in our marriage. When we were younger, it had been fairly easy to walk away from something—when there was so little to walk away from. When it was just the two of us and everything we owned could fit into a pickup truck and the backseat of a car, a move to a new town or a change to a new job wasn't too daunting. Now there was a mortgage, three kids ranging in age from nine to fifteen, and the prospect of spending an entire year without an income in order to "apply" for a job that was already filled by someone who was prepared to spend several million dollars to keep it.

In order to survive, we cashed in a life insurance policy and liquidated funds from an annuity, and I picked up freelance communications jobs so that we could keep food on the table and pay the bills. Miraculously, we were never late in payment on anything and we managed to survive, although there were many months when I wasn't sure how this had been possible. To this day, I find it stunningly stupid when columnists and pundits suggest that I entered politics for the money. Their ignorance of the real journey is staggering.

It was several years into my term as governor—several years after my initial run for office—before my income finally equaled what I had made as a pastor in Texarkana. Arkansas has the lowest salary for its governor of any state in the nation. I clearly didn't do it for the money. It was only because I had the opportunity to write books during my term as governor that I was able to get my kids through college without having to borrow a fortune, and it wasn't until my presidential campaign ended and I started working in television and radio again that my income increased to anything really substantial.

Life inside the fishbowl of politics is unlike what most people can imagine. Every aspect of one's life is open for inspection—tax returns, sources and amounts of income and expenditures, medical conditions, academic records, personal activities, and even friends and relationships. Most of the reporters who are indignant when there is the least attempt to keep some area of life private would never accept or tolerate what they demand of candidates and officeholders, and they would of course argue that they are simply holding us accountable since we are getting a taxpayer-funded paycheck. Fair enough, but their words and opinions will directly affect how people feel about those candidates and elected officials, and perhaps it might be nice to know how much money *they* have and where it comes from; what organizations *they* are members of; what relationships *they* have; what stocks *they* own; and what business relationships *they* have. I know that isn't going to happen, and it probably shouldn't, but the self-righteous I-have-a-right-to-demand-information attitude is often very difficult to tolerate knowing that most of the reporters who ask such questions would never answer them if the tables were turned.

Each Christmas is a time to reflect back on the year behind and to look forward at what lies ahead. We looked back in a very emotional review of not just a year but a career and a comfortable life that was coming to an end. We were looking ahead at the most uncertain since we had had to face Janet's cancer. There was no bridge behind us. We were walking the high wire with no net underneath us. There was a real risk of losing our house, our savings, and all that we owned. No one guaranteed us anything. But we were as much at peace with it all as if we had known the outcome was going to be better than imagined.

We learned from that process to keep things really simple. It was truly starting all over. We were forced to decide what was important in life and what things were just excess inventory. When the dust settled, what mattered was faith, family, and freedom. We would end up losing many things over the next few years, such as our privacy, our financial security, and our nice evenings at home, but we still had what mattered most. Simple things. And we rediscovered them during a transition at Christmas. A simple Christmas.

11.

Faith

My dad never finished high school. Neither did his father or his grandfather or any other male in my family before him. So the fact that I graduated from high school made me the Starship *Enterprise* of my family—I had gone where no man had gone before. Graduating from college was an even bigger achievement. That doesn't mean my father was unintelligent, although it wasn't until I was married and had kids that I came to realize that having an education doesn't automatically make you smart.

On the campaign trail, I often described my dad as the kind of guy who lifted heavy things and only knew hard work. In addition to his job as a fireman, he worked as a mechanic, running a little generator repair shop on his days off, so his hands were always rough and deeply embedded with motor residue, no matter how hard he scrubbed. When I was growing up, the only soap we had in our house was Lava soap, and I was in college before I found out that it isn't supposed to hurt when you take a shower. So many refined ladies go to a spa these days and have an "exfoliation." A bar of Lava soap will do the same thing—for a fraction of the cost!

Mark Twain once said, "When I was a boy of fourteen, my father was so ignorant I could hardly stand to have the old man around. But when I got to be twenty-one, I was astonished at how much he had learned in seven years." It's that way for most of us, I suppose. We grow up thinking that we'll be nothing like our father, that he "just doesn't get it," and then one day we look in the mirror as adults and are startled to see him staring at us. I'm so much like my father that sometimes, when I say or do something like him, my wife and kids will say, "There you go, Dorsey." On a side note, you may be wondering about my father's name. I've often wondered about it myself. His full name was "Dorsey Wiles Huckabee," and the only explanation I've ever been able to come up with for why my grandparents named him that is that they must've wanted to toughen him up—like the dad in "A Boy Named Sue" by Johnny Cash. I never knew exactly where the name came from, but I'm pretty sure my dad spent a good deal of his time with his fists balled up, taking on some punk who was giving him a hard time about his name.

My dad had a great sense of humor, although I don't think I realized that until I was grown. Kids never think their parents are really very funny or entertaining. Of course, my kids still don't think I'm very funny or entertaining, but I've fixed that by cutting them out of any inheritance until they acknowledge the wonderful world of humor that I've imparted to them. No laughs, no loot. I think that's fair.

Storytelling was a big part of our lives when I was little. We didn't think of it as storytelling at the time, just as my father's many recitations of his life and the lives of our relatives. I'm pretty sure that many of the stories were embellished and details were added or changed over time, but it was a part of our world and about the only real family history we had. It's caused me to realize just how important oral traditions can be and the value of a family passing on the heirlooms of their heritage by way of stories.

I wasn't so conscious of such things as a child, but as I grew older, I realized that my dad lived with some regrets and even embarrassment about not finishing school and not having enough money to give us things others had. I eventually would realize that one of the reasons he pushed my sister and me to excel in all we did was that he wanted to make sure that we took advantage of all the opportunities we had. He encouraged us to play musical instruments, to try out for plays, to run for class office, and to play sports. He never forced any particular activity on us, but if we showed interest, both he and my mother would insist that we do our best. If I heard that phrase once, I heard it a million times. "Son, we don't care what you do as long as you *do your best.*" A halfhearted effort, whether in a science project or a household chore, was never acceptable. All endeavors had better be accomplished with a sense of expeditious excellence, although neither of my parents would have used those words. They were old school in that they believed we were to respect authority whether we wanted to or not. That meant teachers, police officers, anyone deemed our "elders," or just about anyone else for that matter.

Getting in trouble at school was never a good thing, but it became unbearable if my parents found out. If the teacher or principal said, "Do you want me to call your parents?" I suddenly became better behaved than Mother Teresa and Mahatma Gandhi combined. On those occasions when they did find out, I never even tried to blame the teacher for being too harsh or perhaps mistaking me for the *real* offender in the class. I was guilty, the teacher was right, and I would go right back to school and apologize. Then they would speak the words I hated most: "You better not let me hear about this again." Of course, I had no intention of my parents' ever *hearing* about it again, though that wasn't to say I wasn't going to *do* the same thing again. I was prepared to keep secrets better than Dick Cheney and would have rather been waterboarded by the CIA than face my parents' wrath for acting up at school.

You might think that since I became a pastor, I grew up in a really religious household, but my dad never went to church. Ever. He didn't want to talk about it, either. He didn't mind that my mother would take my sister and me to Sunday school, as long as we didn't bug him about going. He was not antireligion and didn't speak disparagingly of "church people," but we knew not to bring up the subject. I was a teenager before I found out that the reason my dad was averse to all things church was because once, when he had attended some years earlier, someone had made fun of him for not having the "right clothes." It hurt him deeply, and instead of just ignoring the utterly insensitive and unchristian attitude of the idiot who said it, he allowed that incident to drive him into a deep shell when it came to anything spiritual. I never knew who the wonderful "Christian" was who had uttered such an intemperate remark, but because of that haunting knowledge, I have forever been mindful of how hurtful or how helpful words can be.

My mother was forced to be the spiritual leader of the family, and she was somewhat timid in faith, largely due to the lack of support she got from my dad in all religious matters. For the most part, we went to Sunday school and that was it. "Big church," as we called it, was the morning worship service, and we would go occasionally, but I found it very intimidating because the preacher screamed and scared the daylights out of me. Plus, the music didn't exactly make my motor turn, since it was old-fashioned, piano-banging Southern gospel, and I was really getting into the Beatles. Bob Harrington, a famous evangelist prominent in the sixties, said it best: "More people are following the Beatles than the Baptists, because the Beatles look like they are going somewhere and the Baptists look like they are sorry they've been!"

I did go to the things that were targeted more toward kids, like vacation Bible school in the summers, church camp, and the children's programs for Christmas. In fact, it was at vacation Bible school when I was ten years old that I became a believer. My sister had attended on Monday, but I had refused, saying that it was for girls and sissies. (Like father, like son!) My sister, always the great actor, said that at vacation Bible school, I could get all the cookies I could eat and all the Kool-Aid I could drink and the guys played baseball during the recess.

Based on that description, I decided I would go the next day and quickly discovered my sister's big lie. They didn't let me eat more than two cookies or drink more than one small paper cup full of Kool-Aid. But that didn't matter, because something else did happen that day that changed my life.

It was August 24, 1965, my tenth birthday. So far my birthday and VBS had been very disappointing, and I wasn't prepared for them to get any better. The pastor of the church, Clyde Johnson, came to our class and talked to us about "knowing Jesus." I couldn't really figure out what all that meant, but as he talked, I was so concentrated on what he was saying that I felt as if everyone else in the room had been dismissed and I was there alone. He told us that God knew everything there was to know about each of us. That both scared and excited me. It scared me to think that God knew not just my public words and actions but also my private thoughts. But it excited me to contemplate the idea that the Creator of the universe was actually aware of my existence and, more important, cared about me. I knew that most people in my little hometown didn't know who I was, but the fact that God did was rather overwhelming. Pastor Johnson asked us to raise our hands if we wanted to pray and ask Jesus to come into our hearts. I felt certain that if I lifted my hand, he would call me out and I would be put on the spot and likely humiliated. So I didn't raise my hand, but I snuck in by keeping my hand down but my heart up and prayed the prayer anyway. And though no one else heard me, God did, and I was overwhelmed with a sense of His presence. It wasn't just my physical birthday that day, but my spiritual one as well. In many ways, it was like Christmas, because I received the ultimate gift from God, and I learned that Christmas was all about God's coming to us—not our coming to Him.

The church I attended during my childhood was the Garrett Memorial Baptist Church in Hope, Arkansas. It was a small Missionary Baptist church, which is different from Southern Baptist mainly in denominational structure and the fact that Missionary Baptists tend to be stricter and frown upon everything from dancing to "mixed bathing" (this meant boys and girls couldn't swim together or shower in the same stall, which really would have been scandalous) to "modern music." They lightened up somewhat on the music in later years, but their basic formula was "Get saved, go to church while you live, and go to heaven when you die." There wasn't much discussion about my faith transforming my daily life in terms of my actions or attitudes toward things except for the external activities like going to church, giving tithes, and singing hymns.

During my early teen years, the church hired a youth director who was supposed to create programs that catered to the youth and kept us interested in church. We actually got to play guitars, sing music that sounded closer to what we listened to on the radio, and talk about things that actually mattered to us, like dating, war, drugs, and career choices. This made me willing to go to "big church," so I started going to the Sunday night services because that's when the youth activities were held.

When I was fifteen, I was selected to represent Arkansas at the Hugh O'Brian Youth Foundation Space Seminar at Cape Kennedy, Florida. One student from each of the fifty states and ten from foreign countries were invited to spend a little over a week at no expense at Cape Kennedy to train with astronauts, learn about the space program, and become "Space Ambassadors." While there, I was stunned to find out that most of the other students lacked even a basic belief in God and that most of them were at the top of their class and among the brightest in their state. I came back from that event with a new awareness of what a small world I had lived in and within a week had dedicated my life to Christian service.

I told my parents about my decision, and the next week, none other than my own father came to church for the first time I could ever remember. He said, "If my son is going to do church work, I guess I had better at least go myself." And with that began a new chapter for him and for the rest of the family.

Whatever had kept him out of church before was forgotten, and now nothing could keep him away. He had a hard time understanding the King James Version of the Bible, but my sister, mother, and I bought him a Living Bible, which is a modern-language version that reads more like a daily newspaper in simple, easy-to-understand language.

For the first time in my life, my parents sat together in church, and soon church became the center of their social lives as well as their spiritual lives. It was so strange to see my father going to church that on Sunday mornings I sometimes wondered, "Who is this guy hurrying around the house telling us to get ready so we won't be late to church?"

Over the next few years, I saw my father's spiritual life grow. Slowly but steadily, he came to learn what it means to "follow Jesus," and while those of his generation were generally not overly vocal about such personal things as faith, he became very expressive about his faith. He didn't talk about it too much or buttonhole people on the street, but his actions changed and truly reflected service and sacrifice. Without grudging, he gave with increasing generosity to the church and to special needs he knew about. He was the first to volunteer to mow the lawn of a family whose head of household was ill or to help someone who had to move furniture or to sit with a sick person at the hospital to relieve an exhausted family member.

As my sister and I graduated from high school, moved on to college, and married and started our own families, my father continued to be increasingly active and involved, which proved that he wasn't simply "doing the church thing" for our benefit but was doing it because something genuine had happened to him that had changed his life.

As my sister and I were growing up, my dad really wasn't able to teach us much about faith, trust in God, or preparing for eternity. That all changed at Christmas of 1995.

In 1983, my dad had suffered a heart attack and had had to undergo heart bypass surgery. That was a real turning point in his life as he faced his own mortality in a profound way. From that point forward, he truly felt that every day was a "borrowed day," and he seemed to have a renewed sense of how temporary life is and a determination to make the most of it. One by-product of the experience was that he truly believed that every Christmas was his last one, and each year from 1983 forward, we had to listen to his annual declaration that "this is probably my last Christmas with you guys, so I want to make the most of it." He was so convinced that each Christmas was the last one that we joked among ourselves that this Christmas was the tenth annual "last Christmas" for Dorsey Huckabee.

In 1995, we finally had reason to believe him. He had called us just two days before Christmas and calmly and soberly told us that he had been to the doctor and been told that a melanoma that he had had removed thirteen years earlier had returned and that it was already spreading. There was no crying or whining or complaining on his part. In fact, he was rather matter-of-fact about the news and just wanted us to know that there really wasn't much to be done about it and that he probably only had months left to live.

After all the years of his announcing to us that this was his "last Christmas," this time, we knew it probably really was.

I think there is, for most of us, a sense that Christmas makes us think about our own mortality. If a loved one has died during the year, we can't help but think of the empty chair at the dinner table or the familiar greeting, perennial gift, or other tradition that is missing. We ponder to ourselves what impact our absence would have on the family if we weren't there next year. Because Christmas is the one day of the year that we typically share with our extended families, the loss of a member creates a very definite void and a painful and poignant reminder of the changes that will be permanent.

After all those years of joking about my father's perennial "last Christmas," there was nothing to laugh about this year. The only member of the family who seemed to be handling it with complete equilibrium was my dad. It was almost as if he were relieved that after years of wrongly predicting his demise, the odds of his hitting it right this time were pretty good. My mother had been in very poor health since January of 1992, when she suffered a brain aneurysm and subsequent stroke.

She had slowly regained many of her functions and facilities but was never the same. With this news, it was apparent that they would need to move into an assisted-living facility, as she needed daily care that he could no longer provide.

The fact that he was losing his health, his home, and his life seemed not to have an effect on his demeanor, other than to give him more of a reason to try to keep the rest of us cheered up and optimistic. He reminded us in every conversation that he had lived a good and blessed life and was so very grateful for the years he had had and the joy he had received from seeing his kids grow up, get through college, and have families of their own. We all wanted to comfort him, but he would have none of it—he wanted no sympathy and refused to let us get all weepy and sentimental. He was determined to face this demon head-on and beat it not by outliving it, but by not letting it ruin the time he had left.

Janet and I had gone through her cancer, but it was obvious from the beginning that this was an untamable monster that would take out my father's body, but he was determined that it wouldn't take out his soul. For the next three months, as his body weakened, his faith strengthened. I found myself amazed that this same man who wouldn't even set foot in church for the first fifteen years of my life, and who even as an adult had been somewhat guarded and timid in his outward expression of faith, was now abounding in encouragement as he truly exhibited what it was to "walk through the valley of the shadow of death" and "fear no evil."

With each phone call or visit with my father, I could tell he was physically declining but advancing in his hope and optimism.

He had no illusions of getting well. This was not the kind of man to cling to an unrealistic hope, and he openly told us that he knew he would die soon. His only concerns were for my mother, my sister, and me. He reminded us daily that things were fine with him and that he only regretted that he didn't get to live long enough to see his grandkids grow up and get married.

I was lieutenant governor of Arkansas at the time, having been elected in a special election in July 1993 and then reelected in 1994. In 1996, I had announced my candidacy for the United States Senate for an open seat vacated by Senator David Pryor, and I was leading in all polls and seemingly on my way to victory. The governor, Jim Guy Tucker, had been indicted and was awaiting trial on felony charges related to the Whitewater investigations led by Kenneth Starr. I was confident that no Arkansas jury would ever convict a sitting Democratic governor of anything, especially if the person who would take the office was a Republican. That's why I proceeded with the Senate campaign.

My dad told me, "Son, I wish I were going to live long enough to see you become governor." I told him that he would have to live a very long time, since that didn't appear to be in the works, and I explained to him that even though Governor Tucker was facing trial, it didn't seem likely that he would be convicted, and even if he were, he'd probably refuse to resign until he had exhausted his appeals. In a rare moment for my dad, who seldom tried to instruct me in the nature of politics, he smiled and said, "You will be governor. I just won't be here to see it."

He was right about both.

He died on the last day of March of 1996. He had requested

that I speak at his funeral service, which I did. I was reluctant to do so because I knew that it was going to be hard to control my own emotions, but it was the last thing he had asked me to do for him and it was the last time I would be able to honor one of his requests.

On July 15, 1996, I was sworn in as the forty-fourth governor of Arkansas. Jim Guy Tucker had been convicted in late May and announced that he would resign on July 15. I decided that it was my duty and responsibility to fill the remaining two and a half years in the governor's office rather than continue the pursuit of the Senate seat, and so I withdrew from the race in order to devote myself to the job of governor. The state needed stability and continuity in that office; otherwise we would have had four different people hold the office within a four-year period.

I often wished so very deeply that my dad could have lived another one hundred days to see me become governor. He had taken me to hear a speech by then-Governor Orval Faubus when I was eight years old and Faubus was making a rare appearance in our part of the state. I never forgot what he told me. "Son, I'm going to take you to hear a talk by the governor. You might live your whole life and never get to meet a governor in person." Little did he know I would become one.

I would have loved for my dad to spend at least one night in the Governor's Mansion, because it would have been such a treat for him. That Christmas, our family gathered at the Governor's Mansion to celebrate. We were all there—my sister and her family; our kids; my mother. Only my dad didn't make it, but we left an empty chair at the table in his honor.

On the day I was sworn in, one of my longtime friends from Hope said, "Mike, I sure wish your dad could have been here to see this."

I said, "I believe he did see it. And I think he saw it from the best seat in the house."

I now can laugh when I think about my dad's warning of his imminent demise each year at Christmas. In fact, I laugh at a lot of things when I remember him. But when I think of the Christmas that really was his last, I don't laugh, but I don't cry either. I smile in gratitude not only for a father who gave me life and did everything he could to teach me how to live but also for all he did to teach me how to die. It's easy to leave behind a legacy when you're a governor or when you're famous and everyone knows who you are. But my dad was a simple man, and he left a legacy behind him through his faith, hope, and compassion that I will hold with me for the rest of my life. And even on his last Christmas, he was able to see the joy and happiness that God had blessed him with. He made it a great Christmas. A simple Christmas.

12.

Rewards

July 15, 1996, was like Christmas in July in a very real way. On that day, I was sworn in as the forty-fourth governor of Arkansas after having served as lieutenant governor for three years. I had been elected to serve under the Democrat governor Jim Guy Tucker in 1993 and reelected in 1994 for a four-year term that I didn't get to finish. In late May, Governor Tucker had been convicted of felonies related to the Whitewater scandal and had agreed to step down from his office on July 15. Just minutes before I was supposed to be sworn in, Tucker called me to say he had changed his mind and did not plan to step down after all. This was after seven weeks of transition during which I had prepared to assume the governorship and the state had scrambled to facilitate the changeover. To top it off, the Capitol was overflowing with people who had poured in from around the state to watch the swearing in of the new

Republican governor. All hell broke loose. For almost five tumultuous hours, there were two men—one Democrat and one Republican—claiming to be governor. To make matters worse, the state police and the National Guard were rendered useless because they weren't sure who their boss was. The Democrats controlled the House 89–11 and the Senate 31–4, and yet even they realized that Tucker's actions could sink their party, as the anger and outrage that had started in the Capitol had begun to spread throughout the entire state. Tucker finally relented, resigned unconditionally, and I was sworn in at 7:00 P.M.

As much as I lament the fact that I didn't assume power in a normal, peaceful, and celebratory way, the event was a blessing for me. First, my unlikely and sometimes awkward political journey had taken me to the governor's office, and second, the misconduct of my predecessor meant that the very Democrats who dominated the state were willing to give me—the third Republican governor of Arkansas in more than a hundred years—a fair chance.

Of course, just as the joy and excitement of Christmas morning eventually give way to the challenge of cleaning up the mess you just left under the tree, my celebrations upon assuming office were short-lived. After the first few days of adulation and adoration from the good people of Arkansas, the reality of the job took hold. Being governor is hard work, and it's not a five-day-a-week, nine-to-five job. You have to be on duty 24-7 because a tornado, a prison escape, or the death of a thirteen-year-old boy being held in state custody doesn't always happen during banking hours. But even though it's demanding and challenging, being governor is absolutely the best job imaginable if you are truly interested in changing things and having an impact on society, which is exactly what I wanted to do.

And of course, despite all the hard work, being governor does have its perks, the best being the accommodations. The Governor's Mansion is unlike any other home. Living in it is like living in a very nice bed-and-breakfast where you never have to check out. You are surrounded by people twenty-four hours a day, and there's never a moment when you're completely alone. State police and security detail guard your home at all hours of the day and night. Cameras watch every inch of the property within the gates. If you leave your bedroom in the middle of the night, you always have to make sure you're dressed because there's always a chance you will bump into someone— even at 3:00 A.M.—whether it's a staffer or a group of several hundred people attending an event. But despite the lack of privacy there, the governor's mansion offers every possible convenience. The staff is charged with the task of attending to chores and errands so that the governor and his family can go about their business without the hassle of doing laundry, shopping for groceries, or ironing. I had spent my entire life worrying about money and working hard just to get by. I'd even had to sell my prized guitars just to buy a washer and dryer. Never in my life had I imagined that I'd ever have someone who was hired to do all of my laundry for me!

Even Christmas was an official affair. During the holiday season, the Governor's Mansion serves as the center of activity for the state and plays host to an almost nightly schedule of events, parties, and tours from Thanksgiving until New Year's

Day. It's difficult to separate a private "family Christmas" from the public "citizens' Christmas," and after the first year, my family and I gave up on having a separate "family tree" in the upstairs area where the bedrooms were and instead used one of the several trees that adorned the public spaces downstairs.

Since the earliest days of our marriage, Janet had collected manger scenes that she used to decorate the house. Her favorite was a very large one made of olive wood that we had purchased on one of our many trips to Israel, and during Christmas in the Governor's Mansion, we placed this on a large table in the conference room. She made it her tradition in the mansion to display all of these manger scenes each year. She considered it her way to add a personal touch on the otherwise "official" Christmas decorating process.

Every year, a wonderful group of women volunteers from around the state came to help decorate. They gave several days of their time and much of their care and love to helping make the Governor's Mansion a special and beautiful place at Christmas. No matter how many times I saw the tastefully and carefully planned decorations, I was still in awe of their simple yet stunning beauty.

My entire life, I had searched for the perfect home—first as a newlywed, then as a new father—but during my time as governor, I realized that home is about more than just four walls and a roof. It's about family. Even though I was living in the Governor's Mansion, it was never *my* house. I didn't own it, and I knew that one day I would be forced to move out. I spent a decade sitting on furniture I didn't own, dining off dishes that weren't mine, and eating food I hadn't purchased or cooked.

But my wife and three kids made it feel like home, especially at Christmas.

My family spent more years and celebrated more Christmases in the Governor's Mansion than in any other residence we'd lived in for thirty-five years. Each year was special and marked by a beauty and comfort we hadn't experienced before. That ended with my last Christmas as governor.

My ten-and-a-half-year term came to an end in January 2007, and so the Christmas of 2006—complete with the traditional staff, cabinet, and state agency holiday events—was much more nostalgic and emotional than any before. The pace and pressure of my term had certainly taken its toll on my team, and photos from the last few months of my term reveal just how much we had weathered. We all certainly felt a genuine mood of satisfaction and fulfillment for all we had accomplished over the past decade, but the sense of finality was marked by deep sadness among our staff.

While my family, my staff, and I tried to soak in each moment and savor the memories, we were also faced with a looming deadline to vacate the capitol and the Governor's Mansion. We had determined back in 1996, at the very beginning of my term, that we would do everything we could to make sure this transition was as smooth as possible. I had assumed office in the midst of chaos and confusion, and I had promised myself that I wouldn't force my successor to deal with the same thing.

When I walked into my office on my first night as governor, I was shocked and appalled by the mess waiting for me. The previous administration had left no files, records, or even phone books behind, and the only thing that remained was a half-full drawer of papers for our legal counsel. There were no records of appointments, no budgetary records for any state office, and not even instructions on how to use the phones. We were able to get records of appointments from the secretary of state and budget information from the finance and administration department, but for everything else we had to start from scratch. It was a petty thing to do, and it meant that I had to spend a good chunk of my early days in office just trying to get organized, when I should've been running the state. I wouldn't let the next guy suffer through that.

But despite my attempts to facilitate a smooth handover, certain journalists and opponents began to accuse me of destroying hard drives and office computers. In fact, I *did* have the hard drives from several of the computers removed and destroyed, but only *after* my staff and I had salvaged all records of transactions, budgets, appointments, and important correspondence that my successor might need. The procedure we followed was not only authorized and recommended by our department of information services but based on federal guidelines for information protection. In many cases, state-owned computers were sold to outside parties, and if files weren't sufficiently scrubbed, hackers could obtain sensitive information—even medical records and Social Security numbers—that, if dropped in the wrong hands, could lead to privacy violations or lawsuits against the state. We made sure all pertinent records and information got passed to the new administration and even placed funds in our budget to help cover costs of the transition and vacated our offices earlier than required so the new guys could come in without a hiccup.

We did the same at the Governor's Mansion. Janet and I moved out two weeks early so as to give the new first family the opportunity to arrange the house to their liking before they moved in. Yet despite the herculean effort we put forth to make things easier, my staff and I were rewarded with a series of shoddily researched news articles and columns and even ethics complaints, all of which were baseless. So the peaceful, relaxing and reflective final Christmas we had hoped to spend in the Governor's Mansion was quite the opposite. And on top of the political drama, I still had to contend with some issues at home.

Janet had been experiencing pain in both of her knees for some time. The trouble was caused by a combination of old basketball injuries and the residual effects of her cancer surgery, which had led to neuropathy in her legs. Her doctor told her that her left knee needed to be replaced immediately and she would need to replace the right knee before too long, so Janet decided to have both operations at the same time—two days before Thanksgiving, just in time for the annual Christmas events and our preparations to move.

Having one knee replaced is tough, but getting both replaced on the same day is pretty much unbearable. If you ever find out that someone has given me double knee surgery, call the authorities and report medical malpractice because I assure you that I would never elect to have that done.

Janet was virtually incapacitated for the entire holiday season and during our move to a home we had purchased in North Little Rock, so I was pretty much left to do the packing on my own. We had accumulated a substantial amount of stuff over our thirty-two years of marriage, and much of what we had brought to the Governor's Mansion more than ten years earlier was still in unopened boxes. The way I looked at it, if we had lived without it for ten years, then we could live without it forever. I voted to get rid of those boxes without even opening them, but Janet had a different idea. I'm sure you know she won, and we ended up going through each and every box and taking most of them with us. Most of those are now in storage in our new home.

As we went through our stuff, we put things into four categories: throw away, give away, store away, or move away. I donated all of my official papers and memorabilia to my alma mater, Ouachita Baptist University, as I had agreed to do, but I gave away a large number of keepsakes from my tenure and various mementos that had accumulated through the years. (Most of these things—like photos of special events—went to my staff.) I decided, after much hesitation, to dispose of my rather extensive theological library, which I had started in high school and had grown to include several thousand books. I donated the entire library to the Chaplain's Ministry at the Arkansas Department of Corrections in the hope they might inspire some inmates to turn their lives around.

Everything else—besides the truckloads (literally) of stuff we threw away—came with us. In the weeks leading up to the move, I woke up almost every morning between 4:00 and 5:00 A.M. to take a Suburban full of boxes, which I had packed late the night before, over to our new house before returning to my office for a long day of more transitional work.

Oh, and in the middle of all this I was also in the process of trying to determine whether I was going to run for president of the United States, and I had a new book called *From Hope to Higher Ground* coming out the week I left office. Just a few things to keep me busy and occupied!

So just how simple was my Christmas? I had to take care of a wife rendered a complete invalid; tidy up after ten years as governor; move out of the Governor's Mansion and into a new home; launch a new book; and decide whether to run for president. Oh, and I still had to deal with all of the normal Christmas stuff—shopping, decorating, etc.—and the parade of state-run events. I was sure looking for some "peace on earth, goodwill toward men"!

But a couple of days before Christmas, it all hit me—in so many ways, my life was better than I could have ever imagined it. In my frazzled condition, I had forgotten that Christmas wasn't a time for me to become an irritable and impatient tyrant because I was stressed out and so many things were going wrong. It was the one time of the year that I needed to stop my motors and listen to the quiet and reassuring voice of God reminding me that, no matter how crazy life got, I would always have the original Christmas gift—His love, salvation, and hope.

I paused to reflect on that first Christmas and what it all meant. God had wanted to send us a message, and He could've done it by shouting from the mountaintops or sending a flood or a burning bush our way. He could've had a party or a press conference or a parade. But He didn't. He sent a baby. A baby who would carry God's whole message in His very essence. A baby who cried and had to learn how to walk and talk and who had to grow up the way all of us do—one year at a time. There would come a time in that infant's life when throngs of thousands would line the streets to either cheer Him with shouts of "Hosanna!" or jeer Him with shouts of "Crucify him!" People would surround Him just to ask for a prayer or the chance to touch His garments. He would go on to change the world and the lives of millions forever. But He started as a baby.

God could have sent His son into this world fully grown and ready to start performing miracles. But it was the years of patient preparation that made the last part of the journey not only tolerable but in fact rewarding. Over the years, surely there were times when the young carpenter in Nazareth must have prayed, "Father, the world's a mess. Don't you think it's time I go forth and start my ministry?" At times, I'm sure He felt frustrated when the answer from above was, "No, I need you to make some more chairs. Maybe another table." Jesus, who knew that His real purpose on earth was to bring people to God by preaching great sermons, performing amazing miracles, recruiting disciples, and eventually giving his life on a Roman cross, was stuck building furniture for the first thirty years of his life. Seems like an awful waste of talent! But God knew that the preparation was more important than the presentation, and on that day just before Christmas in 1996, I began to realize that all spiritual pilgrimages are marathons, not sprints.

I have run four marathons, so I know what it's like not only to run one but also to train for one. Before I decided to train for my first one, I would never have deemed it possible that I could endure *watching* a marathon, let alone running one. For my first marathon, I trained for eight months. It was grueling and tedious work, but when the time came to actually run the marathon, I discovered that the hard part wasn't running that actual 26.2 miles in one stretch; it was preparing for it. In the end, my hard work had paid off.

Jesus didn't show up on earth running at full speed. He showed up as a helpless infant who had to be carried, fed, and held by someone else, just like every other baby. It took Him thirty years of preparation and virtual silence and solitude before He ever preached His first sermon or performed a miracle. But that waiting and training and patience prepared Him for the last three years of His life, during which He carried out God's mission on earth and received the greatest reward—and gave us the greatest gift—imaginable.

I started thinking about the amazing journey I had already had. I thought back through the many Christmases I had as a kid, when I would patiently wait all year for the big day and when it finally came, I would be thrilled just to get one gift I really wanted (even though I had looked at dozens of things in the Sears catalog). The only Christmas stress I had to endure was hurrying to rewrap the packages that my sister and I had broken into. I thought about trekking through the woods with my dad to find a little tree at my uncle's farm that we could chop down and bring home to decorate.

But here in 2006, things were a lot more stressful. But I realized that I needed to stop thinking about how much I was stressed and start thinking about how much I was *blessed*. I had married my high-school sweetheart and was still married to her after thirty-two years, a battle with cancer, and the birth of three kids, none of whom we were supposed to have. I was the governor of my state, even though my dad had always told me that I might never even *meet* a governor. I was in the process of trying to figure out what to do with all the stuff I had accumulated over the years, even though just a few decades earlier I had been able to fit everything I owned into the backseat of a car. My wife and I were in the process of moving again, but this time we were moving into a nice, large house of our own instead of the duplex we had lived in when we were first married. Janet was recovering from knee surgery, but she was alive—thirty-one years longer than we thought possible. I was trying to make a tough decision about my next career move, but that move might be a step toward becoming the next president of the United States.

Life might not seem so simple, but it was good! Very good. And I realized it was good because the slow and steady ramp I had climbed to get to where I was had given me perspective on what an amazing journey it had been.

Christmas started taking on its true meaning again. I decided that all the things that stressed me were really the unimportant things. The important thing at Christmas was the simple truth that God loves us. He loves us when we have nothing and loves us when we have a lot. This is a better gift than anything your family, your friends, or even Santa can bring you.

Over the next fifteen months, I would experience the ride of my life in my campaign for president. It was a tough and grueling process, but reporters often commented that I seemed to be enjoying it, and I was even dubbed the Happy Warrior by some columnists who noticed that I didn't appear to be overwhelmed by the pressures and rigors of the campaign.

I would always remind them that I considered myself the luckiest man in America. I knew where I came from, and yet here I was, running for president—where else but in this country could that be possible?

I think the Christmas of 2006 was a transformational event for me—after years of getting busier and taking on more responsibility than ever, I was able to recapture the original spirit of Christmas and was reminded that a great Christmas isn't the expensive one or the elaborate one. It's the simple one. The one in which we are reminded that God continues to choose to speak to us through the simple things that no amount of money can buy. It's what He tried to teach us. And if we listen, He's still saying it now. You might not hear it in the noise of a Christmas party or see it in the stunning, bright lights of Times Square, but you might just hear it slightly above the sounds of cows and sheep in a little grotto in Bethlehem. A baby cries. God is speaking. It's a simple message. But it's a saving message. So this year, I hope you have a warm Christmas, I hope you have a joyful Christmas, but most of all I hope you have a simple Christmas.

Acknowledgments

Adrian Zackheim of Portfolio and Sentinel imprints contacted me about doing a Christmas book. When a Jewish publisher says he's interested in a politician's doing a book about Christmas, you just gotta listen!

Like my previous (and hopefully future projects) with Portfolio and Sentinel, this has been a sheer delight. The entire publishing team, and especially project coordinator and editor Brooke Carey, have been rugged taskmasters to keep me on their ridiculously tight deadlines, but they did it with a spirit that makes me want to sing "Joy to the World" in July. Okay, maybe it wasn't *that* lovely, but they really are not only the very best in professionalism, but also truly fun to work with. Their suggestions to make the book better were always helpful, yet they never attempted to change my thoughts or my words. After you read it, maybe you will have wished they had!

Acknowledgments

Frank Breeden and Duane Ward of Premiere Authors are the best I know in not only handling all the logistics of getting me lined up with the publisher, but also in putting together the best promotional plan possible to make it a worthy endeavor for the author, the publisher, the bookstores, and outlets.

The Sentinel and Premiere publicity teams—Will Weisser, Allison McLean, Christy D'Agostini, Laura Clark, Josh Smallbone, and Joel Smallbone—really helped promote this book. Three weeks on a bus is a long time, but they made it as comfortable and as smooth as possible. And the bus crew at Premiere who outfitted the bus with a little studio so I could do my radio commentaries for the ABC Radio Network while on the road.

And most of all for the most important person in the entire process, *you* the reader. I hope you enjoy the book. If you have half the fun reading it as I did remembering and reliving the stories behind it, then it will have been a great success.

And it just seems appropriate to say, "Merry Christmas!"

Read on for the first chapter from *Dear Chandler,*
Dear Scarlett, available now in hardcover.

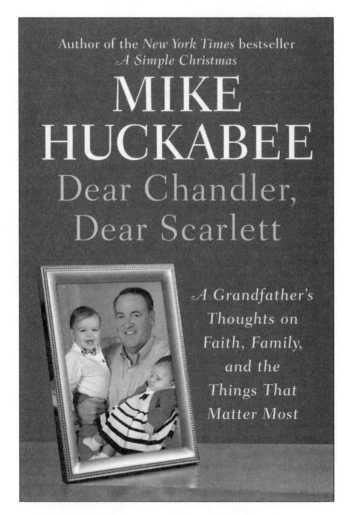

Author of the *New York Times* bestseller
A Simple Christmas

MIKE HUCKABEE

Dear Chandler,
Dear Scarlett

*A Grandfather's
Thoughts on
Faith, Family,
and the
Things That
Matter Most*

ISBN 978-1-59523-093-5

CHAPTER ONE

On Parents

Dear Chandler, Dear Scarlett:

Whatever you thought when you saw your parents for the first time, I promise you it was nothing compared to the excitement your parents felt when they saw you for the first time. You kept them waiting for nine months while they tried to figure out how big you would be, how cute you would be, and, of course, when they'd get to hold you and smother you with love.

Parents are a pretty important part of who you are because, without them, you wouldn't be here in the first place. (How that all happens we'll deal with later—your parents are hoping *much* later.) A parent's job doesn't end after you're conceived and born, though. You will find your mother and father very helpful in your early days, especially before you can walk, talk, feed, or clean yourself after you've engaged in the most elementary bodily functions.

And even if you didn't need your parents to provide your food, shelter, clothing, and medical care, you'd still want them around because they are incredibly entertaining. You must find it pretty funny when they talk to you in a baby voice, trying to explain things you can't possibly understand. "Does baby want to go to sleepy land?" I always thought it would be hilarious if God in His infinite sense of humor gave infants the ability to sit up in their cribs and declare, "No, I don't want to sleep—I just got here and I'm ready to PAR-TAY!" Talking to babies is kind of like talking to dogs. "Does Fluffy want to go for a walk?" Just once I want to hear a puppy say, "Not right now. I want to finish watching *Old Yeller* on cable."

The reason your parents talk to you like this is because they are actually losing the ability to have a rational adult conversation. They just don't know it. As funny as this is, you need to have some sympathy for them because ever since you came into the world, they've spent most of their time feeding you, clothing you, cleaning you, changing your diaper, putting you to bed, and protecting you from cold viruses and grandparents. And even when they're not doing these things, they're thinking about doing them, or dreaming about doing them, or talking about doing them. So, basically, you've taken over their brains.

And let me tell you, this distraction can often lead parents to do some pretty dumb things.

Before your uncle John Mark was born, I knew I would be totally new to the parenting thing and didn't have the first clue what I'd be doing. I spent months reading every book I could get my hands on about how to take care of a baby. By the time the baby came, I thought I was basically ready for anything—from his stepping on a rusty nail to breaking his arm to throwing a tantrum in public. What I wasn't prepared for was being thrust into a life-or-death situation that would forever change my understanding of fatherhood.

One day I was standing over John Mark's crib when he was just a few days old, changing his diaper, when suddenly his chest collapsed. It happened so quickly, and even though his chest quickly returned to its original position, I was worried. What had just happened did not look natural. Then, before I could scream for his mother, an ambulance, or perhaps the national guard, it happened again. When I saw my baby son's tiny little chest cave in a second time, I mustered all the volume I had in my voice and yelled to your grandmother, "JA-NET! COME HERE NOW! CALL 911! JOHN MARK IS HAVING A HEART SEIZURE!" I continued my pan-icked cry for help until your grandmother arrived. Just then, John Mark's chest collapsed again. "That is a hic-cup," your grandmother calmly informed me before walking out of the room and leaving me to my diaper-changing duties.

"Hiccup? Are you sure?" I called out at her. I thought she was being rather cavalier about our first and only child's possible collapsed lung or cardiac arrest. I had hiccupped plenty of times in my life, and my chest never touched my spine because of it!

But she was right—it was just a hiccup. I had been so worried about having to save my child from a life-threatening injury that I had lost all common sense. So when your parents overreact to some things, as they will, forgive them. No one is great at something on the first try, and parenting requires a person to deal with a whole lot of surprises—some good, some bad. You may laugh at them sometimes (as will I, because I know what it's like), but I promise, if you ever have children, you'll understand.

Beyond providing you with basic economic and physical necessities, as well as twenty-four-hour live interactive entertainment, parents will give you something you need more than anything else: unconditional love.

You probably already know your parents love you. They tell you all the time and they treat you as if you were the center of the universe (which, to them, you are). But it's the unconditional aspect of this love that you probably won't fully grasp until much later on. I hope your parents are still around when that happens so you can tell them you finally understand and let them know how much you love them, too.

Unconditional love means that your parents don't love you because you're cute (even though you are), or because you're intelligent (of course you are!), or because you have amazing talents to sing or play sports (I'm sure you do!). They don't love you because you make their lives easier. In fact, when you first showed up, you were pretty much useless. You couldn't help out around the house, and yet you still demanded constant attention and care. If that wasn't enough, you kept your parents up all hours of the night, and because they had to take care of you all the time, they didn't have time to do a lot of the things they used to do, like go out to eat or have leisurely conversations with their adult friends. You pretty much upended whatever serenity they had.

You certainly aren't loved because of your financial contribution to the family. Your parents would probably never smile at you if they fully understood the costs associated with bringing you into this world. Your parents could shop at fine jewelry stores on a weekly basis and have lobster flown in each Friday from Maine with the money it will cost to properly provide for your every need and desire. With food, clothing, medical bills, day care, and education, not to mention all the hobbies and toys you'll want throughout your childhood, your cost to your parents will be staggering. But even if they got a bill for your next twenty-two years of life support and the cost of your education, they still wouldn't put you on eBay.

No, this love you receive by the truckload is not your parents' way of thanking you because you've proved yourselves economically, politically, or socially useful. Your parents love you simply because you're their children, and that will never change. Nothing you do will make them love you more, and nothing you do will make them love you less. Now, you can do some things that might make them *like* being around you more or less, but their love is pretty well set. Even if you break their hearts (and you'd better not!), they will still love you, forever and always.

I'm often amazed my own parents never left me on the doorstep of an adoption agency with a note encouraging some nice family to take me home and try to train me in the art of being a civilized human being. I was so rambunctious, my mother would sometimes ask, "Were you raised by wolves?" "No, not wolves," I told her. "Just you and Dad." That *really* made her mad, but I thought it was a perfectly legitimate response to what seemed like a really ridiculous question.

It's a good thing eBay wasn't around when I was little, because my parents would probably have tried to auction me off for a minimum bid of three dollars. And on some days, that would have been asking too much. Like the day Rosalind Doyle and I got in trouble for throwing rocks at cars driving past our house. Rosalind was my next-door neighbor's granddaughter, and she spent a lot of time at her grandparents' house. She was one day older than me, so we had a connection right off the bat. She was a beautiful young girl, but at age four I didn't care so much about that. All I cared about was that she really knew how to throw a rock. So there we stood in her grandparents' gravel driveway, throwing handfuls of loose gravel at passing cars as hard as our little arms would let us. We thought the sound of rock on metal was pretty cool. And we thought we were pretty cool, too—right up until we pelted the car of the local municipal judge, the Honorable John Wilson. As if that weren't bad enough, Judge Wilson knew my parents, and told them what Rosalind and I had done. Darn the luck! How were we supposed to defend ourselves against a judge? I wasn't going to be able to talk my way out of that one. And I didn't.

In those days, corporal punishment was the preferred method of responding to bad behavior. Today, it's almost unheard of, but when I was growing up, most parents assumed it was the best—sometimes the only— way to send a message and correct deviant behavior. That day I thought my parents were going to extend corporal punishment to make it capital punishment! Fortunately, an old-fashioned spanking (and a good one!) was the limit of the punishment.

While I was growing up, I got more than my share of spankings, and even though I didn't enjoy it, I survived just fine. I eventually came to realize that my parents didn't discipline me because they hated me and enjoyed seeing me in pain. It was exactly the opposite. They disciplined me because they loved me.

I don't expect you'll understand or express gratitude when your parents discipline you. It's never fun to get punished, but that's the point. Your parents discipline you so you learn the consequences of bad behavior now, when your offenses are relatively minor, instead of later, when your bad behavior could lead you to jail, or worse. So whenever your parents tell you, "One day you'll thank me for this!" you might not thank them right away, but, trust me, one day you will.

While we're discussing your parents, you might as well know something about your ancestry. I wasn't sure if I should bring this up, but one day you might run for political office, so it's probably best you hear everything from me rather than read it in the papers. I'll start by saying the same thing my dad (your great-grandfather Dorsey Huckabee) once said to me: "Son, don't look too far up your family tree—there's stuff up there you don't want to see!" He then explained that some of our ancestors were horse thieves, which in the days of the frontier was considered a heinous crime because people needed horses to travel and work the land. I'm not sure I believe this story, however, because my entire child-hood I begged to have a pony. I figured that if my ances-tors were so good at stealing horses, my dad could have at least picked up a pony somewhere. But the best I got was one of those broomstick-like things with a stuffed toy horse head on top. I never did get a real pony.

Your ancestors on my side of the family weren't ex-actly the most impressive folks. They didn't come over on the *Mayflower* or carry the blue blood of European nobility. They were never commissioned by a king or queen of some country to establish a colony of well-dressed, properly educated, and erudite ladies and gen-tlemen. No, my family was more blue collar than it was blue blood. From what we know, the Huckabees arrived on the shores of Georgia in the late 1700s and early 1800s to either avoid or escape the debtor prisons of England. Apparently, they had tried to go to Ireland first, but were turned away. So they booked passage on ships that pretty much dumped them off in a swamp where they learned that fighting mosquitoes was as dif-ficult as fighting the British authorities. But poverty and hardship made them resilient, and a lot of those traits are probably still flowing through you. You'll need them for the world you face, so I hope you've inherited the grit and gravel that helped your forebears survive the tough and tumultuous American frontier. They may not have been well educated, prestigious, or wealthy, but they knew how to survive, and that's all that mattered.

Your grandpa (that would be me) was the first male in our family to graduate from college, but I was also the first to finish high school. My dad would have liked to have gotten a diploma, but in his day an education wasn't as critical for making a living, and usually only the privileged could afford to go to college. When World War II broke out, he went to work in the shipyards in Houston and never finished school. You shouldn't be ashamed of that, though. It took a long time for our family to reach the milestone of a college degree, but now that this path has been established, it will be up to you to make sure you do even better. Your ancestors suffered from poverty and lack of opportunity, but they still managed not only to survive, but also to pave the way for every generation after them to have the things they lacked. If not for them, you wouldn't be here, or, at least, you wouldn't be in such a good situation. You were born into a family who loves you and can take care of you, and you live at a time when you have more opportunity than anyone who has lived before you. Imagine all the things you can do. Your parents and your grandparents are all blessed to have received a college education. You should never take it for granted.

Never be embarrassed by your family history. Like your great-grandfather, I love to joke about the horse thieves, drunkards, gamblers, and all-around rowdies who certainly came before us. But for the most part, the Huckabees were hardworking people who mostly kept to themselves and yet always treated others with fairness and respect. They may not have been rich in pocket, but they were rich in spirit, never giving up on themselves or their communities. Hopefully, some of that same rugged spirit is deep within you. Should you ever run for public office, play sports, or start a business, you'll need it to go forward in the face of hardship and opposition. Without it, you're likely to be walked over while everyone else gets to where they want to go. Somehow, I think you'll both be fine.

But always remember that you had nothing to do with who your ancestors were or what they did. You do, however, have *everything* to do with what *you* decide to do with your life. Cherish the parts of your heritage that are worth holding on to. As for the parts you'd rather forget, the best way to separate yourself from them is to live such a big and wonderful life that people will only remember you for you.

Out of all the things your ancestors gave you, the best was your parents, who in turn gave you the chance to live what will hopefully be a long and joyous life. You are both blessed with really great parents. I know that because half of them were trained for their jobs by me.

Your parents are far from perfect, but one thing I know for sure—they love you unconditionally and totally. They will never abandon you, and while you might disappoint them from time to time, they will always love you no matter what. You will probably get angry at them sometimes, and you'll probably even think they are unfair when they say no, but they used to think I was unfair, too. Now they probably think I was right after all. You might think that yourself someday!